OPPORTUNITY YOUTH

COMMUNITY-LED SOLUTIONS FOR ENGAGING DISCONNECTED YOUTH

SOCIAL ISSUES, JUSTICE AND STATUS

SOCIAL ISSUES, JUSTICE AND STATUS

OPPORTUNITY YOUTH

COMMUNITY-LED SOLUTIONS FOR ENGAGING DISCONNECTED YOUTH

PARIS MARINA
EDITOR

nova publishers
New York

NOTICE TO THE READER

The Publisher has taken reasonable care in the preparation of this book, but makes no expressed or implied warranty of any kind and assumes no responsibility for any errors or omissions. No liability is assumed for incidental or consequential damages in connection with or arising out of information contained in this book. The Publisher shall not be liable for any special, consequential, or exemplary damages resulting, in whole or in part, from the readers' use of, or reliance upon, this material. Any parts of this book based on government reports are so indicated and copyright is claimed for those parts to the extent applicable to compilations of such works.

Independent verification should be sought for any data, advice or recommendations contained in this book. In addition, no responsibility is assumed by the publisher for any injury and/or damage to persons or property arising from any methods, products, instructions, ideas or otherwise contained in this publication.

This publication is designed to provide accurate and authoritative information with regard to the subject matter covered herein. It is sold with the clear understanding that the Publisher is not engaged in rendering legal or any other professional services. If legal or any other expert assistance is required, the services of a competent person should be sought. FROM A DECLARATION OF PARTICIPANTS JOINTLY ADOPTED BY A COMMITTEE OF THE AMERICAN BAR ASSOCIATION AND A COMMITTEE OF PUBLISHERS.

Additional color graphics may be available in the e-book version of this book.

Library of Congress Cataloging-in-Publication Data

ISBN: 978-1-63117-415-5

Published by Nova Science Publishers, Inc. † New York

CONTENTS

PREFACE

The purpose of this book is to provide context on the characteristics of youth who are not working or in school, and the circumstances in which they live.

Chapter 1 – Across the nation, individuals and community groups are working together to find new and effective solutions to local problems. Recognizing that the best ideas do not come from Washington but from communities, President Obama created the White House Council for Community Solutions in December 2010 by Executive Order to encourage the growth and maximize the impact of innovative community solutions and civic participation.

The White House Council for Community Solutions (the Council) was charged with: identifying key attributes of successful community solutions; highlighting best practices, tools, and models of cross-sector collaboration and civic participation; and making recommendations on how to engage all stakeholders in community solutions that have a significant impact on solving our nation's most serious problems.

Executive Order 13560 also directed this diverse group of leaders from various sectors to identify specific policy areas in which the federal government is investing significant resources that lend themselves to cross-sector collaboration. The Council, therefore, focused its attention on the broad question of what drives successful community solutions: those making greater than 10 percent progress on a metric. Next it focused on applying these findings to create substantial opportunity for disconnected youth. The Council chose this often overlooked population because of the untapped potential of these young people and the high cost to our nation. The 6.7 million disconnected youth cost our nation approximately $93 billion in direct and indirect social costs in 2011 alone, making this issue both compelling and urgent. While all youth have potential, connecting these youth to education or employment will change the trajectory of their lives, as well as benefit their community and our nation as a whole.

Chapter 2 – Policymakers and youth advocates have begun to focus greater attention on young people who are not working or in school. Generally characterized as "disconnected," these youth may also lack strong social networks that provide assistance in the form of employment connections and other supports such as housing and financial assistance. Without attachment to work or school, disconnected youth may be vulnerable to experiencing negative outcomes as they transition to adulthood. The purpose of the report is to provide context for Congress about the characteristics of disconnected youth, and the circumstances in which they live. These data may be useful as Congress considers policies to retain students in high school and to provide opportunities for youth to obtain job training and employment.

Since the late 1990s, social science research has introduced different definitions of the term "disconnected." Across multiple studies of disconnected youth, the ages of the youth and the length of time they are out of school or work for purposes of being considered disconnected differ. In addition, a smaller number of studies have also incorporated incarcerated youth into estimates of the population. Due to these methodological differences, the number of youth who are considered disconnected varies. According to the research, the factors that are associated with disconnection are not entirely clear, though some studies have shown that parental education and receipt of public assistance are influential.

This Congressional Research Service (CRS) analysis expands the existing research on disconnected youth. The analysis uses Current Population Survey (CPS) data to construct a definition of "disconnected." This definition includes noninstitutionalized youth ages 16 through 24 who were not working or in school at the time of the survey (February through April) and did not work or attend school any time during the previous year. The definition is narrower than those used by other studies because it captures youth who are unemployed and not in school for a longer period of time. This is intended to exclude youth who may, in fact, be connected for part or most of a year. Youth who are both married to a connected spouse *and* are parenting are also excluded from the definition. For these reasons, the number and share of youth in the analysis who are considered disconnected are smaller than in some other studies. Still, 2.6 million youth ages 16 through 24—or 6.9% of this population—met the definition of disconnected in 2010, meaning that they were not in school or working for all of 2010 and at some point between February and April of 2011. As expected, rates of disconnection have varied over time depending on economic cycles.

Like the existing research, the CRS analysis finds that a greater share of female and minority youth are disconnected, and that their rates of disconnection have been higher over time. The analysis evaluates some other characteristics that have not been widely studied in the existing research. For instance, compared to their peers in the general population, disconnected youth tend to have fewer years of education, and are more likely to live apart from their parents and to have children. Disconnected youth are also twice as likely to be poor than their connected peers. The analysis further finds that the parents of disconnected youth are more likely than their counterparts to be unemployed and to have lower educational attainment.

Given the state of the current economy, rates of disconnection may remain stable or climb. Policymakers may consider interventions to reconnect youth to work and/or school. Interventions can target children and youth at a particular stage of their early lives. Interventions can also focus on particular institutions or systems, such as the family, community, and schools.

In: Opportunity Youth
Editor: Paris Marina

ISBN: 978-1-63117-415-5
© 2014 Nova Science Publishers, Inc.

Chapter 1

COMMUNITY SOLUTIONS FOR OPPORTUNITY YOUTH[*]

The White House Council for Community Solutions

President Barack Obama
The White House
1600 Pennsylvania Avenue, NW
Washington, DC 20500

Dear Mr. President:

It is a great honor and privilege to submit to you the report of the White House Council for Community Solutions (the Council), *Community Solutions for Opportunity Youth*. When you created the Council by Executive Order in December 2010, you asked the Council to help identify and raise awareness of effective community-led solutions to our nation's most serious problems. The Council engaged in intensive factfi nding and listening efforts and ultimately chose to address an area of critical importance to America's future: putting every young person on a clear path to economic opportunity.

During today's challenging economic times, too many families and communities across the country are struggling to make ends meet and to

---

[*] This is an edited, reformatted and augmented version of a Final Report, dated June 2012.

simply do more with less. In fact, the unemployment rates for young Americans—who are typically less skilled and new to the workforce—are at historic highs.

However, your administration's commitment to creating jobs for Americans is moving the needle and helping create new opportunities for all Americans to get back on track. The Council's work complements other administration efforts by focusing on creating opportunity where it is needed most: in support of opportunity youth.

The Council concluded that it could draw attention to the promise of these young people and the actions that can tap their potential to contribute to our economy and society. The Council sees these young people—the 6.7 million 16 to 24 year olds (roughly one in six in this age group)—who are disconnected from both school and jobs as opportunity youth. Through our outreach efforts, we heard directly from and were struck by the tremendous response from citizens, cities, and community and corporate partners around the nation who stand ready to take action and do something to help make a difference in the lives of these young people.

Opportunity youth are isolated from the paths that can lead to economic independence. Moreover, the cost to the nation of inaction is high. According to a study commissioned by the Council, when lost revenue and direct costs for social supports are factored in, taxpayers will shoulder roughly $1.6 trillion over the lifetimes of these young people. Absent action, their futures are at risk—and collectively our nation's future prosperity is put at risk.

The report presents recommendations for successful community-led solutions across the nation: driving development of more successful community collaboratives to harness the potential of these young people; creating shared national responsibility and accountability; engaging youth as leaders in the solution; and creating more robust on-ramps to employment. We know that with training and support, opportunity youth hold enormous promise to infuse our economy with new skills and leadership, and they are eager to accept responsibility for their lives. The Council believes that the actions identified in this report, coupled with a nationwide awareness of the issue, will lead to significant progress toward putting all of our young people on a path to prosperity. At a minimum, we believe implementing the Council's recommendations will lower the number of opportunity youth by 10 percent.

On behalf of the members of the White House Council for Community Solutions, we thank you for this opportunity to identify and address a matter of critical importance to the nation.

Patricia Stonesifer
Chair
White House Council for Community Solutions

White House Council for Community Solutions
1201 New York Ave., NW
Washington, DC 20525

Dear White House Council Members:

Thank you for inviting us to review this report and contribute to its innovative recommendations for actions to improve the lives of the nation's opportunity youth.

As young people who have faced challenges in our lives, we don't often have the opportunity to be heard. When we first became part of the National Youth Ambassadors program organized by the Youth Leadership Institute (YLI), we were not sure that our opinions would matter.

As we contributed to the Council's work and developed our skills as spokespeople and leaders, we discovered that our voices do in fact matter a great deal. The highlight was having the opportunity to provide input on the draft of the final report recommendations and to see our ideas incorporated in the final report.

This note is our way of expressing our appreciation for the chance to have our say. We now know that our opinions, experiences, and stories do matter, and that our ideas, solutions, and work in our community will make a difference. The three of us who attended the Summer Jobs+ Summit earlier in the year were moved by the experience. At that event, and in the months since, all Youth Ambassadors have become part of the national conversation on how to help opportunity youth get connected to education and employment pathways that ensure success and allow us to contribute to our families and our communities. As highlighted in the report, young people can and want to be part of designing community solutions to the challenges we face.

In closing, we want to say that we know the work does not stop here. We look forward to inspiring other youth to be problem solvers in their communities, and to ensuring that there is "no decision about us, without us."

Sincerely,
The YLI Youth Ambassadors

Jairus Cater, Nashville, Tennessee
Ryan Dalton, New Orleans, Louisiana
Trevor Easley, Columbus, Ohio
Francisco Garcia, Hacienda Heights, California
Torres Hughes, Chicago, Illinois
Shaakirah Medford, New York, New York

Jose-Luis Mejia, San Francisco, California
Brian Nguyen, Seattle, Washington
Hannah Sharp, Indianapolis, Indiana
Brittany Woods, La Mirada, California
Hashim Yonis, Minneapolis, Minnesota

LIST OF COUNCIL MEMBERS

First Lady Michelle Obama, Honorary Chair,
White House Council for Community Solutions
Patricia Stonesifer, Chair,
White House Council for Community Solutions, philanthropic advisor
Byron Auguste, Director, Social Sector Office, McKinsey & Company
Diana Aviv, President and CEO, Independent Sector
Paula Boggs, retired executive, Starbucks; philanthropist; musician
Jon Bon Jovi, musician, Bon Jovi; Board Chair,
Jon Bon Jovi Soul Foundation
John Bridgeland, President and CEO, Civic Enterprises
James Canales, President and CEO, James Irvine Foundation
Scott Cowen, President, Tulane University
John Donahoe, President and CEO, eBay Inc.
Michael Fleming, Executive Director, David Bohnett Foundation
David Friedman, Director and Chair,
Edison Properties/HNB Private Trust
Jim Gibbons, President and CEO, Goodwill Industries International, Inc.
Michele Jolin, Senior Fellow, Center for American Progress
Michael Kempner, Founder, President and CEO, MWW Group
Steven Lerner, Founder and Managing Partner, Blue Hill Group
Maurice Miller, Founder and CEO, Family Independence Initiative
Laurene Powell Jobs, Co-Founder and Board President, College Track
Norman Rice, CEO, Seattle Foundation

Kristin Richmond, Founder and CEO, Revolution Foods
Judith Rodin, President, Rockefeller Foundation
Nancy H. Rubin, Board Member, National Democratic Institute
Paul Schmitz, CEO, Public Allies
Jill Schumann, Principal, ParenteBeard LLC
Bobbi Silten, Senior Vice President,
Global Responsibility Gap Inc.; President, Gap Foundation
Bill Strickland, Founder and CEO, Manchester Craftsmen's Guild
Laysha Ward, President, Community Relations and Target Foundation;
Board Chair, Corporation for National and Community Service

INTRODUCTION

Across the nation, individuals and community groups are working together to find new and effective solutions to local problems. Recognizing that the best ideas do not come from Washington but from communities, President Obama created the White House Council for Community Solutions in December 2010 by Executive Order to encourage the growth and maximize the impact of innovative community solutions and civic participation.

The White House Council for Community Solutions (the Council) was charged with: identifying key attributes of successful community solutions; highlighting best practices, tools, and models of cross-sector collaboration and civic participation; and making recommendations on how to engage all stakeholders in community solutions that have a significant impact on solving our nation's most serious problems.

Executive Order 13560 also directed this diverse group of leaders from various sectors to identify specific policy areas in which the federal government is investing significant resources that lend themselves to cross-sector collaboration. The Council, therefore, focused its attention on the broad question of what drives successful community solutions: those making greater than 10 percent progress on a metric. Next it focused on applying these findings to create substantial opportunity for disconnected youth. The Council chose this often overlooked population because of the untapped potential of these young people and the high cost to our nation. The 6.7 million disconnected youth[1] cost our nation approximately $93 billion in direct and indirect social costs in 2011 alone, making this issue both compelling and urgent. While all youth have potential, connecting these youth to education or employment will change the trajectory of their lives, as well as benefit their community and our nation as a whole.

In its outreach and listening sessions, the Council discovered these young people have energy and aspirations and do not view themselves as disconnected. To the contrary, they are eager to participate in their communities, in fact, to own the development of their lives. They want to create a successful future but need the tools and opportunities to create that success. To acknowledge their untapped potential, the Council chose to refer to this population as opportunity youth.

The Council approached its work in three phases:

Phase One: Fact-finding and listening efforts to establish knowledge base. *(December 2010-June 2011)*

The Council reviewed data-driven research and conducted extensive outreach to understand successful community-based groups of organizations working together (community collaboratives) and the demographics, needs, and existing programs for opportunity youth. The most compelling input came from young people themselves, but the Council also spoke with more than 300 organizations, families, mentors, businesses, social sector organizations, and government agencies that serve youth. The Council also conducted site visits to community collaborations that are achieving significant progress on persistent community issues.

Phase Two: Leveraging knowledge base to develop and launch resources. *(June 2011–January 2012)*

In fulfilling elements of the Executive Order, the Council identified gaps in information and resources to support community solutions. As a result, the Council developed the following resources to build awareness and assist communities. (All resources are available at http://www.serve.gov/council resources.asp#maincontent.)

- *Community Collaboratives Toolbox.* Includes best practices, tools, and models for effective collaborative approaches.
- *Employer Tool Kit: Connecting Youth to Employment.* A simple guide for employers to create a mutually beneficial youth engagement program.

- *The Economic Value of Opportunity Youth.* A report on the size of the population of opportunity youth, the cost of inaction to taxpayers and society, and the benefits of reinvesting in these young people.

Phase Three: Building awareness, shining the spotlight on what works, advocating for greater systemic change to support success, and listening to feedback. This knowledge was used to develop the Council's recommendations to the President. *(January 2012–June 2012)*

> The Council worked across sectors to build awareness of the data, tools, and the path forward through personally leveraging a wide variety of media opportunities, participating in Opportunity Community Conversations hosted by more than 30 United Way local affiliates, and participating in a White House Youth Summit to bring youth, key leaders, and change-makers together to commit to action.

Through its work, the Council has fulfilled its mandate and presents in this report its key findings and resulting recommendations to drive the creation of more successful collaboratives in communities across the nation. This report also provides an assessment of opportunity youth in our nation, as well as four core strategies – driving the development of successful cross-sector community collaborations, creating shared national responsibility and accountability, engaging youth as leaders in the solution, and building more robust on-ramps to employment – with accompanying recommendations for reconnecting these youth to successful careers and civic lives that will benefit themselves as well as their communities and our nation as a whole.

EFFECTIVE COMMUNITY SOLUTIONS

Consistent with the administration's view that the most innovative, effective solutions come not from the federal government but from communities themselves, the Executive Order directed the Council to identify key attributes of effective community-developed solutions to our national problems.

Recognizing that despite good intentions and examples of success, most community efforts fail to achieve significant results, the White House Council for Community Solutions worked with The Bridgespan Group to identify collaboratives that have actually moved the needle, or created more than a 10 percent improvement on a community-wide metric, to understand what makes them effective, and to determine whether these key characteristics could be adopted by other communities seeking greater impact. The analysis identified a dozen communities across the country where all sectors have pulled together to make more than 10 percent progress on a community-wide metric, and more than 100 additional communities that are making progress in this direction.

> We have to recognize that to transform young people's lives, it's not individual programs or individual interventions; it's communities and supportive relationships.
>
> *– Paul Schmitz CEO, Public Allies*

Individual nonprofit services can be fragmented and dispersed, with each organization typically serving a limited population with specific interventions. Funders then measure success at the organizational level, rather than the broader community level. These individual efforts are critical to the lives and well-being of the people they serve and are important examples of success to demonstrate that progress is possible. But overall, these approaches are not resulting in significant change at a community-wide level, which is frustrating to all: taxpayers, funders, policy makers, service providers, and the beneficiaries themselves.

America has a long history of community revitalization efforts that were groundbreaking and changed the lives of many individuals, helping shape the work of successful efforts today. Communities can point to numerous examples of collaborations created to solve local problems. But only recently have we begun to see needle-moving collaboratives that are data-driven and highly focused on aligning existing resources toward a common set of targets for community-wide change.

To better understand these collaboratives, The Bridgespan Group and Council members conducted extensive research to understand this work and inform its recommendations, including a review of more than 100 high-potential collaboratives, site visits to a number of community collaboratives that have achieved significant needle-moving change, interviews, and a day-long meeting with leaders of community collaboratives and national organizations that support their work.

To ensure evidence-based results, each profiled collaborative underwent a structured due diligence process. This involved external research and exploratory conversations with the collaborative followed by site visits or in-depth discussions. While the Council sought to be inclusive in its search, the resulting list of proof points is not exhaustive.

Through this research, the Council developed a Community Collaborative Framework (see Exhibit 1) that serves as a road map for success for other communities across the country to effect large-scale change.

Based on these findings, the Council believes that community collaboratives with these identified attributes should be replicated to address complex, persistent social issues in communities across the nation.

Exhibit 1. Effective Community Solutions

CORE PRINCIPLES	CHARACTERISTICS OF SUCCESS	SUPPORTIVE RESOURCES
What type of collaborative are we talking about?	What do successful collaboratives have in common?	What do they need to thrive?
Collaboratives with: • Aspiration to needle-moving (e.g., 10 percent +) change on a community-wide metric • Long-term investment in success • Cross-sector engagement • Use of data to set the agenda and improve over time • Community members as partners and producers of impact	• Shared vision and agenda • Effective leadership and governance • Deliberate alignment of resources, programs and advocacy toward what works • Dedicated capacity and appropriate structure • Sufficient resources	• Knowledge • Tools • Technical assistance from peers/experts • Policy • Funding

Core Principles of Needle-Moving Collaboratives

In addition to sharing a commitment to needle-moving change, these collaboratives had the following operating principles in common:

- Commitment to long-term involvement. Successful collaboratives make multi-year commitments because long-term change takes time. Even after meeting goals, a collaborative must work to sustain them.
- Involvement of key stakeholders across sectors. All relevant partners play a role, including decision-makers from government, philanthropy, business, and nonprofits, as well as individuals and families. Funders need to be at the table from the beginning to help

develop the goals and vision and, over time, align their funding with the collaborative's strategies.

- Use of shared data to set the agenda and improve over time. Data are central to collaborative work and are the guiding elements for collaborative decision-making.
- Engagement of community members as substantive partners. Community members are involved throughout the process in shaping services, offering perspectives, and providing services to each other, not just as focus group participants.

Community Collaborative Success: Increasing High School Graduation and College Enrollment Rates

The Strive Partnership, a cross-sector collaboration focused on "cradle-to-career" education, has achieved an increase of 10 percent on high school graduation rates and 16 percent on college enrollment since 2006. Cincinnati's students were falling behind in college readiness, with Ohio ranked 42nd in the nation for bachelor's degrees. The president of the University of Cincinnati joined KnowledgeWorks, a community foundation, and the local United Way to understand the problem and plot a path forward. They created Strive, made up of multiple collaborative networks, linked to an overall student road map of success, and outlined research-based milestones for kids from cradle to career. A shared vision, deep research, and data-driven planning and evaluation were several important factors that made the program succeed. Strategically aligning existing resources against cradle-to-career needs has led to 40 of the 54 identified indicators moving in a positive direction with several including college enrollment rates increasing by more than 10 percent.

White House Council for Community Solutions. *Case Studies of Effective Collaboratives.* 2011. http://www.serve.gov/new-images/ comm_collabs_ case_studies.pdf

---

Characteristics of Success of Needle-Moving Collaboratives

After conducting deeper research into the 12 needle-moving collaboratives, five common elements emerged as essential to their success. (See Exhibit 1)

- Shared vision and agenda: finding the common denominator. Developing a common vision and agenda are two of the most time-consuming and challenging of all the tasks a community collaborative undertakes. They are also two of the most vital. Establishing quantifiable goals can catalyze support and build momentum, and developing a clear road map can help organizations look beyond narrow institutional interests to achieve community-wide goals.

- Effective leadership and governance: keeping decision makers at the table. Successful collaboratives need a strong leader to fully engage stakeholders and coordinate their efforts. The biggest challenge is not so much bringing decision makers to the table, but keeping them there for years of hard work ahead. To achieve such a feat, it is important for the collaborative's leader to be respected highly by the community and viewed as a neutral, honest broker. In addition, the leader must work to create and maintain a diverse, inclusive table where both large organizations and small grassroots organizations have powerful voices.

- Alignment of resources toward what works: using data to adapt continually. Regardless of their breadth, successful collaboratives pursue a logical link among the goals they seek, the interventions they support, and what they measure to assess progress and success. Collaboratives are required to be adaptive, adjusting their approaches based on new information, changes in conditions, and data on progress toward goals. At times, collaboratives may push for new services to fill in gaps. But much of the work of successful collaborations focuses on "doing better without spending more," or getting funders, nonprofits, government, and business to align existing resources and funding with the most effective approaches and services to achieve their goals. In many cases, this will mean working together to target efforts toward particular populations, schools, or neighborhoods rather than operating in a more ad hoc manner.

- Dedicated staff capacity and appropriate structure: linking talk to action. Having dedicated staff is critical to success, as is having a staff structure appropriate to the collaborative's plan and goals. There is no predetermined right size. Effective staff teams can range from one full-time strategic planning coordinator to as many as seven staff for more complex, formalized operations. In general, dedicated resources focus on convening and facilitating the collaborative, data collection, communications, and administrative functions.

- Sufficient funding: targeted investments to support what works. Collaboratives require funding both to maintain their dedicated staff and to ensure that nonprofits have the means to deliver high-quality services. Even though the first job of most collaboratives is to leverage existing resources, in every needle-moving collaborative studied, there was at least a modest investment in staff and infrastructure. This investment often included in-kind contributions of staff or other resources from partners. Sustainable funding itself becomes one of the collaborative's key objectives, as does "funder discipline"– sticking with the plan rather than developing individualized approaches or continuing to fund activities that are not part of the strategy.

Community Collaborative Success:
Reducing Teen Pregnancy

Teen Pregnancy Prevention Oversight Committee, a nonprofit-led collaborative, resulted in a 31 percent drop in the teen birthrate over five years. In 2006, Milwaukee had one of the highest birth rates among teens in the United States. Convened and staffed by the United Way of Greater Milwaukee, the collaborative was co-chaired by the editor of the local Milwaukee paper and the health commissioner. Together, they set an ambitious goal to reduce the rate by 46 percent by 2015. Leadership and governance were critical elements: as a trusted and neutral party organization with its own staff and funds, the local United Way was positioned uniquely to convene the group. The 31 percent drop in the birth rate to date is significant as national rates have been steady, and the local poverty rate has increased dramatically with the recession.

White House Council for Community Solutions. *Case Studies of Effective Collaboratives.* 2011. http://www.serve.gov/new-images/ comm_collabs_case_studies.pdf

---

Supportive Resources

The concept of collective impact has been growing over a number of years. However, when members of The Bridgespan Group convened leaders in collaboration, they pointed to several gaps in knowledge and tools. Building on the substantive work of pioneering collaborative efforts that launched the evolving field of collective impact, the Council chose to focus its efforts on these gaps: life stages of a community collaborative; best practices within each stage; dedicated capacity required for success (in terms of staff time and talent, committees, oversight, etc.); and best practices in community engagement for greater impact.

Community Collaborative Success: Reducing Violence

Operation Safe Community, a local government-led collaborative, reduced violent crime by 27 percent and property crime by 32 percent over five years. The city of Memphis, Tennessee, struggled with violent crime in 2006, and ranked number one in the nation. Operation Safe Community was launched by the district attorney to bring law enforcement and other sectors together to address the issue by setting specific goals, establishing baseline data, and developing detailed plans in 15 areas. As a result, the murder rate is the lowest in 30 years.

White House Council for Community Solutions. *Case Studies of Effective Collaboratives.* 2011. http://www.serve.gov/new-images/ comm collabs case studies.pdf

---

As a result of these articulated needs, the Council developed specific tools and a set of 12 case studies of collaboratives that have demonstrated change for all communities interested in launching or enhancing existing collaborative efforts. These resources are available at www.serve.gov.

Community Collaborative Success: Improving Elementary Test Scores

Parramore Kidz Zone (PKZ), a neighborhood-based education collaborative, resulted in a 15 percentage point jump in reading and 21 percentage point jump in math for elementary students performing at or above grade level.

Parramore was Orlando's toughest neighborhood when Buddy Dyer became the city's mayor in 2003. Data painted a bleak picture of the 1.4-square-mile neighborhood adjacent to downtown Orlando. Percentages of elementary students scoring at or above grade level on the FCAT, Florida's standardized test, were 45 percent in English and 27 percent in math in 2007.

> Mayor Dyer provided effective leadership and governance by aligning resources toward what worked and treating the community as partners in determining strategies to address this issue. PKZ now uses community feedback and survey results to design programming. Another key to PKZ's success is the use of data to drive the agenda. PKZ now uses teen pregnancy rates, reading and math proficiency scores, readiness for school by kindergarten indicators, and juvenile arrest rates to gauge its progress and direct its efforts.
>
> Both reading and math scores have improved dramatically to 60 percent and 48 percent, respectively. And while Orlando's overall juvenile crime rate declined by an impressive 67 percent from 2006 to 2010, Parramore showed significantly better results with an 81 percent reduction.
>
> White House Council for Community Solutions. *Case Studies of Effective Collaboratives.* 2011. http://www.serve.gov/new-images/ council/pdf/comm_ collabs_case_studies.pdf

FOCUS ISSUE: OPPORTUNITY YOUTH

The Council focused on opportunity youth as the issue of critical national importance where the complexity and urgency of the problem requires coordinated effort to make meaningful progress. In applying the framework of successful community collaboratives to the problem, the Council first conducted research to better understand this population of young people.

Understanding Opportunity Youth in Our Nation Today

The Number of Opportunity Youth Is Large and Diverse

As the nation strives to boost our economic competitiveness—and to put every American on a path to success—too many young adults (one out of six) are disconnected from education and work.

- In the summer of 2011, the unemployment rate of youth 16 to 24 years old was more than 18 percent or twice the overall unemployment rate; for young African Americans and Hispanics it was 30 percent and 20 percent, respectively.[2]

- Opportunity youth represent diverse socioeconomic backgrounds. While being disconnected is both a consequence and cause of poverty, many of these young people come from families of moderate means. In fact, while three out of five opportunity youth reported that they grew up in a poor or working class family, the other two said their families were middle class or better.

Youth Are Ready and Eager to Be a Part of the Solution

Council listening sessions and United Way Opportunity Community Conversations found that disconnected young people are assets and need to be supported to address their challenges, but are often not engaged by decision-makers. These youth want to be actively involved in developing solutions for themselves. A recent report, *Opportunity Road: The Promise and Challenge of America's Forgotten Youth*, by Civic Enterprises and America's Promise Alliance in association with Peter D. Hart Research Associates, confirmed the Council's findings. This study included in-person interviews with 613 disconnected youth in 23 locations across the United States in August 2011. Survey respondents were between the ages of 16 and 24, in numbers representative of the population as a whole in terms of gender and race/ethnicity who are currently out of school, out of work for at least six months, have no college degree, are not disabled, not incarcerated, and are not a stay-at-home parent with a working spouse.[3] Key findings included:

- Opportunity youth are optimistic. Despite their challenges, 73 percent are very confident or hopeful about achieving their goals, 85 percent want a good career and job, 67 percent want a college or technical degree, and 65 percent have a goal to finish high school or college and know they can achieve it.
- Opportunity youth accept responsibility for their futures. Some 77 percent believe that getting a good education and job are their own responsibilities.
- Opportunity youth want to reconnect to work, school, and service, but they need help.
- The top obstacles that youth face to reconnecting to work are as follows: no jobs are available where they live (51 percent), or they don't have enough work experience (50 percent) or education (47 percent) to get the job they want. But nearly one-third (32 percent) said that they do not know how to prepare a resume or how to interview.

- The top obstacles to reconnecting to school are as follows: cost is more than they or their families can afford (63 percent); they need to make money to take care of their families (48 percent); and they do not have transportation or they need to work and cannot balance work and school (40 percent in each case). Nearly one-third (32 percent) say no one showed them how to apply to college or helped them figure out how to pay for it.
- Opportunity youth point the way to reconnecting. Some 79 percent want to connect with successful peers they can relate to, to college professors (69 percent), and to business mentors (65 percent) to get help going back to school and work; 78 percent want job opportunities that enable them to earn some money and attend school at the same time ("Learn and Earn").
- Opportunity youth want to improve life for others. Nearly seven in ten (69 percent) want to make a difference improving life for others, while only 3 percent report they are volunteering in their communities, suggesting their disconnection from school and work is impeding their desire to give back.

These young people offer an opportunity for an infusion of potential leadership and productivity in our workforce and economy—and they are eager to accept this responsibility.

The Cost of Inaction Is High
The need for broad national action and collaboration among business, nonprofit, and community leaders is urgent. Consider that in 2011 alone, taxpayers shouldered more than $93 billion to compensate for lost taxes and direct costs to support young people disengaged from both education and work. In their analysis *The Economic Value of Disconnected Youth*, researchers found that, over the lifetime of this group, the cost to society is estimated to be $4.7 trillion.

- Lifetime earnings are diminished with each missed year of work equating to two to three percent less earnings each year thereafter. And significant gaps in the education-work sequence of activity lead to pay and employability handicaps.
- Over a lifetime, an opportunity youth's earnings are estimated to be $375,000 compared with a high school graduate's of $712,000.[4]

There Is Opportunity to Make a Real Impact

In addition to the value of getting these young people back on the road to successful lives, our country is facing a large skills gap that can be addressed partially by tapping the potential of this cohort of Americans. Nearly two-thirds of job openings in the next decade will require some postsecondary education.[5] To fill these jobs, the United States will need to accelerate its progress and produce three million more students who graduate with a postsecondary degree by the end of this decade.[6] Furthermore, to achieve the President's goal to lead the world in postsecondary attainment by the end of this decade, we need to produce eight million more graduates than we currently expect to produce.

> All the solutions don't come from the programs themselves, they really come from all of the support systems, and we need everybody on board. We need the parents, we need the friends, we need the entire community.
>
> *– Maurice Miller; Founder and CEO, Family Independence Initiative*

Understanding the Needs of Opportunity Youth

In beginning its work, the Council did extensive outreach and research to understand the demographics, needs, and existing programs for opportunity youth. The following visual (Exhibit 2) provides a snapshot of the diversity of this population in terms of their degree of preparation for, as well as their ability to take up, opportunities.

In summary, the number of opportunity youth is large, and the impact of their status is not only on the individual, but also on the nation and requires an all-in effort to make progress. While both prevention and intervention are critical to the solution, the Council focused its efforts on those already disconnected as they are often overlooked and have great potential. The needs of opportunity youth are complex and diverse, thus the solutions require a multi-sector approach to create multiple paths of opportunity to reconnect.

Exhibit 2. Opportunity Youth Segmentation

Opportunity youth can be segmented
based upon their degree of preparation and ability to take up opportunities.

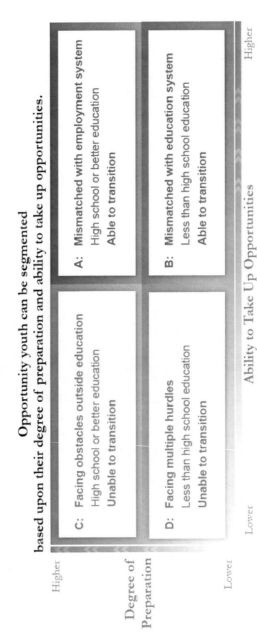

Exhibit 3. Needs and Supports Required

(Illustrates how the diversity of needs translates to a wide variety of individualized support required.)

The needs of opportunity youth are diverse and we must meet them 'where they are' ...

——— Types of employment opportunities open to youth increase along this spectrum ———

	GROUP D Facing multiple hurdles	GROUP C Facing obstacles outside education	GROUP B Mismatched with education system	GROUP A Mismatched with employment system
Critical Needs	• Integrated services across education, social supports, and employability	• Wraparound supports • Alternative pathways to learning & employment	• Pathways to GED/high school completion • Alternative training and credentialing programs	• Employment pathways & more advanced credentialing opportunities
Types of Support Required	• Opportunity for education within a stable set of interventions (Group C needs) • Move youth a step 'up the ladder' on path to full employability	• Food access • Housing & transport • Health/mental health services • Life skills mentoring • Daycare • Financial/legal literacy • Alternative pathways to GED, diploma, or community college	• High school graduation support • GED support • On the job training and work-based learning programs • Alternative credentialing programs • Afterschool/summer programs	• Community college collaborations • Certification/ credentialing programs • Internship or apprenticeship opportunities • Starter jobs

Fundamental Principles Underlying Recommendations

Through its research, the Council developed three fundamental principles to guide all strategies addressing the needs of opportunity youth:

1) **Young people themselves are key to the solution.** Research shows that opportunity youth have informed views of what works for them and their peers.
2) **All sectors must pull together in the same direction to address the challenge.** The barriers facing opportunity youth are complex and cannot be solved by families, communities, schools, employers, nonprofits, or the government alone. To see dramatic, measurable progress in the lives of opportunity youth requires the engagement of all sectors pulling together in the same direction to provide the diverse range of services needed.
3) **Policies and funding must be data-driven to ensure limited resources are invested wisely.** Policy and funding decisions need to be guided by accurate data about opportunity youth and effective interventions to meet their needs and challenges to ensure the most effective use of limited funding.

CORE STRATEGIES AND RECOMMENDATIONS

Opportunity youth reside throughout our nation. Without support from individuals, community leaders, and government, they may fail to bridge to successful careers and civic lives that will improve their own futures as well as those of their communities and our nation. The good news is that strong examples of success exist. While not an exhaustive list, the Council believes the following four strategies and recommendations have the potential to make significant progress on community-based issues and specifically toward ensuring more of our nation's young people are on the path to prosperity:

- Drive Development of Successful Cross-Sector Community Collaboratives
- Create Shared National Responsibility and Accountability
- Engage Youth as Leaders in the Solution
- Build More Robust On-Ramps to Employment

Strategy One: Drive the Development of Successful Cross-Sector Community Collaboratives

Cross-sector community collaboratives that actually move the needle—realize at least a 10 percent change in the problem they aim to address—share a select set of attributes and must be replicated increasingly across the nation.

Research and practice have shown that reconnecting opportunity youth is difficult, if not impossible, within the bounds of a single intervention. The exception to this is when this single intervention is not really a single program, but a collaboration of services brought together around the needs of the youth.

Examples of success already mentioned in this report such as the Strive Partnership and Parramore Kidz Zone have proven that outcomes for youth can be improved dramatically if cross-sector assets are aligned around the needs of the youth. In addition to these already successful collaboratives, other early efforts are also under way. The United Way Worldwide responded to the President's call to action by convening a series of Opportunity Community Conversations. Affiliates across the country brought together diverse stakeholders to discuss how communities could address their community's opportunity youth needs and shared the results of these conversations with the Council. While many of the hopes and concerns voiced were similar across the country—safe places, access to opportunity, positive role models, or mentors—many of the communities also described unique assets that could be leveraged and made a commitment to begin collective action.

Key Recommendations

1) **Prioritize Funding for Best Practice Cross-Sector Community Collaboratives.** Public and private funders should prioritize successful collaborative efforts that exhibit best practice characteristics. We *strongly support the $20 million Disconnected Youth Initiative proposed in the President's 2013 budget.* The departments of Education, Health and Human Services, and Labor are proposing a total of $20 million to develop interagency strategies to strengthen the impact of federal programs serving opportunity youth and identify opportunities for enhanced flexibility and collaboration. This initiative would take the lessons from the administration's Promise Neighborhood and Choice Neighborhood initiatives that support place-based collaborative activities in communities across the

country, as well as from other collaborative efforts such as the Department of Justice and Department of Education's National Forum on Youth Violence Prevention, and adapt the work to promote collaborative work focused specifically on opportunity youth.

2) **Promote Collaborative Use of Data Across Agency Lines.** Given that the ability to access and share data across systems is critical to successful solutions for complex social issues, the administration should allow local communities access to critical data across the continuum of a young person's life, improve the connection between federal, state, and local data sources, and provide clarity about the ability to share data. This increased access must be consistent with the intent of relevant privacy laws and ensure the responsible use of data. We recommend that the administration:

- Align funding for state and local data systems. The administration should *encourage states and localities to provide more flexibility in existing programs to build, adopt, or adapt data systems and to connect disparate data collection efforts that receive federal funding.*

- *Propose changes to the Family Educational Rights and Privacy Act (FERPA).* FERPA was written originally before personal computers were invented, and it now creates barriers to the responsible use of data across agency lines. We applaud the Department of Education's new guidance interpreting the FERPA legislation and call on the administration to go further by recommending changes to the legislation itself. More immediately, relevant agencies and their privacy attorneys should provide more helpful guidance, promising practices, and tools (i.e., sample memorandums of understanding and consent forms) for sharing data among agencies for opportunity youth.

3) **Align Policies to Reduce Fragmentation, Improve Efficiency, and Achieve Better Results.** Communities often have multiple, fragmented efforts to address complex issues, each governed by a separate federal policy that makes it difficult to align services into a coherent strategy. The administration should *simplify and align eligibility criteria, uses of funds, and reporting requirements across programs and agencies to allow coordination of services.* We applaud the President's Memorandum on Administrative Flexibility and strongly support the $113 million Performance Partnership Pilots for Disconnected Youth proposed in the President's 2013 budget. These

pilots should improve outcomes for opportunity youth by supporting state, regional, or local efforts to align funding from several different federal sources into coherent, efficient, and effective paths to prosperity. Pilot sites will be given the flexibility from federal regulations necessary to work across agency lines to achieve better efficiency. In areas where pilots are successful, this flexibility should be made widely available.

4) **Create a National Community of Practice.** The nonprofit sector should *establish a community of organizations dedicated to identifying and sharing best practices and developing tools for organizations committed to creating opportunities for opportunity youth.* With focused thought leadership, success could be more easily leveraged and replicated.

5) **Replicate Successful Aspects of Youth Opportunity Grants.** From 2000 to 2005, the Workforce Investment Act's (WIA) Youth Opportunity (YO) grants funded 36 high poverty rural and urban communities and Indian reservations to improve education and labor market outcomes for youth between 14 and 21 years old. YO sites brought education, job training, and wrap-around support services together in a safe, accessible youth community center. An independent evaluation of the more than 90,000 youth participants, released by the U.S. Department of Labor in 2008, found that, while results varied significantly by location and by subgroup, employment impacts were positive for most groups, especially younger youths, blacks, and native-born youths. YO also had a positive impact overall on increasing the percentage of the youth population with at least an 11th-grade education and increasing the percentage in secondary school. We recommend that the administration *encourage funding the successful aspects of YO through WIA.*

6) **Create an Incentive Fund.** The administration should *allow for the use of existing WIA formula funding to create a pilot collective impact fund* for communities that are committed to aligning existing community resources and setting specific targets to reconnect young people to school and work. This fund would be open to all proven programs and provide local communities with $1 million to $1.5 million for three years, to be matched at the local level, with resources to support data collection and other infrastructure for the community collaborative.

The Council believes enacting these recommendations will lead to a significant reduction in the population of opportunity youth through the replication of needle-moving community collaborations focused on their needs.

Strategy Two: Create Shared National Responsibility and Accountability

Shared national responsibility for opportunity youth requires high-level consistent leadership to coordinate efforts across agencies and the collection, reporting, and sharing of rigorous data to shine a national spotlight on who these young people are, what they need, and what they are capable of doing. Shared accountability also requires a clear understanding of available public and private efforts to allocate limited resources to those programs with the greatest return on investment.

As demonstrated in the core principles of successful collaboratives, to create significant progress against a complex social issue, it is critical to create a sense of shared responsibility and accountability from all sectors. Key to creating shared responsibility and accountability are long-term commitment and a data-driven shared vision.

President Bill Clinton created the President's Crime Prevention Council to coordinate federal efforts in support of at-risk youth. President George W. Bush created a White House Task Force for Disadvantaged Youth. President Obama created the White House Council for Community Solutions. To make significant progress on the issue of opportunity youth, there needs to be sustained leadership to coordinate efforts across agencies and to collect, report, and share rigorous data to shine a national spotlight on who these young people are, what they need, and what they are capable of doing.

The ability to understand the reach of an issue and have a consistent commonly defined metric against which to measure progress is essential to making progress on complex social issues. Because there is not a standard definition for this population, and there is not a single statistic or a report that is regularly published in our nation, opportunity youth remain a population below the radar for most national and community leaders and the public. In other countries such as Australia and the United Kingdom, data on so-called NEETs (Not in Education, Employment or Training) has been collected and reported for more than a decade.

With high-level consistent leadership on this issue and a publicly tracked, common metric, it will be possible to assess the range of services supporting opportunity youth and their efficacy, which is essential to creating a coordinated, cost-effective effort to make significant progress.

Key Recommendations

1) **Establish High-level Consistent Leadership**. The need for senior-level prioritization, coordination, and accountability has been demonstrated in recent presidencies. Rather than recreating the function ad hoc in every new administration, we recommend that the federal government *establish an ongoing function, possibly within the Domestic Policy Council, and charge this leadership with creating goals and clarifying responsibilities among agencies for improving outcomes for opportunity youth*. The Council applauds the Department of Education's creation of the Interagency Forum on Disconnected Youth along with the existing efforts of many coordinating bodies including the Interagency Working Group for Youth Programs and the Coordinating Council on Juvenile Justice and Delinquency Prevention. Their work would be better coordinated through a single entity anchored by an annual strategy. This strategy should encompass all efforts on behalf of opportunity youth, set clear goals, and detail how federal resources will be coordinated to achieve these goals.

2) **Lead With Data.** To create greater national, state, and local accountability for reconnecting opportunity youth and to empower communities with the information they need to drive change, the administration should *begin collecting and reporting information regularly on opportunity youth through the Current Population Survey or American Community Survey*. Such information should include the size of this population, demographics, and activities.

3) **Evaluate Current Programs.** To understand the role that the federal government itself plays in reconnecting youth to education and work, the administration should *conduct a comprehensive survey across departments and agencies to understand what programs and initiatives are serving opportunity youth, how effectively they reconnect youth to education or employment, and at what scale*, perhaps through the Interagency Forum on Disconnected Youth. This

evaluation can be used to allocate existing funding to the most effective programs.

4) **Scale Up and Reward Effective Programs.** The fastest way to reconnect opportunity youth is to *support effective programs that have waiting lists of young people eager to transform their lives, but for whom no slots are available.* We encourage the administration to support and Congressional leaders and state and local governments to respond by scaling successful evidence-based programs. The administration should also encourage scaling of successful programs through establishing selection criteria for Pay for Success proposals serving opportunity youth. The innovative Pay for Success funding model provides programs with a guaranteed predetermined amount of funding if they achieve agreed-upon outcomes for the populations they are serving.

5) **Invest in Innovation.** We applaud the administration's Investing in Innovation Fund, Social Innovation Fund, and Workforce Innovation Fund, and we urge the administration to *establish selection criteria for proposals serving opportunity youth and to open eligibility to nonprofit programs.*

Strategy Three: Engage Youth As Leaders in the Solution

Engaging youth as leaders in developing and highlighting solutions that work will create more relevant, higher quality, and increasingly effective programs and resources for opportunity youth.

Youth want their voices to be heard, and they have strong, informed opinions of what will help them reconnect. Young people have a critical stake in the quality and sustainability of the solution as the Council heard in youth roundtables, United Way Community Conversations, and the national survey as presented in *Opportunity Road.*[7]

Youth as Leaders in the Solution:
Higher Graduation Rates

Nashville, Tennessee has raised high school graduation rates by more than 20 percentage points to 83 percent and reduced truancy by 35 to 40 percent.

Youth were involved on every level of this effort, through the youth co-chaired Child and Youth Master Plan Task Force, providing unique insight into solutions. Like many cities, Nashville had an array of programs and initiatives providing services and activities for children and youth, but high school graduation rates hovered around 58 percent, and school attendance was dismal. In February 2010, Mayor Karl Dean, the Mayor's Office of Children and Youth, and community leaders convened a task force to pull together the key people and organizations involved with youth in Nashville—schools, government agencies, businesses, nonprofits, youth, and parents. The Master Plan Task Force organized all youth-focused efforts into a framework and created a shared vision for the community. Using strategies from the Ready by 21 Coalition, the plan articulates desired outcomes for all children and youth for a successful future and acts as a blueprint for people and organizations to work together. Youth and their families were engaged throughout the process, and the Task Force was co-chaired by a senior from a local high school.

White House Council for Community Solutions. *Case Studies of Effective Collaboratives*. 2011. http://www.serve.gov/new-images/ comm_collabs_case_studies.pdf

Specifically:

- Almost 80 percent of opportunity youth want to connect with mentors to whom they can relate, such as successful peers, business mentors, and college mentors.
- Opportunity youth are more likely to respond to reconnection strategies that provide strong, integrated supports and treat youth as part of the solution rather than the problem.

There are many examples of how youth leadership has made programs more effective, including youth-driven solutions in the Chicago public school system and the Nashville Child and Youth Master Plan (see details in sidebars on pages 27 and 28).

When youth are involved as community leaders, the decisions are more relevant, reliable, and more likely to be embraced by them. Perhaps most importantly, their innate understanding of their generation allows them to develop more authentic solutions to the issues they face.

Key Recommendations

1. Formalize Youth Input

- Create a Presidential Youth Working Group. We applaud existing efforts to reflect youth input in the administration via the White House Liaison to Young Americans and the recent White House Young America Series. The administration should expand on these efforts and *establish a Presidential Youth Working Group composed of young people that reflects a diversity of backgrounds and experience, including opportunity youth, to advise the President and his cabinet secretaries on the perspectives of young people*, offer input on how to make federally funded youth programs more effective, and support activities by each department to better engage young people in the policy-making process.
- Call on Leading Organizations in the Nonprofit and Faith-based Sectors to Create a National Youth Council. We applaud coordinating efforts of existing organizations and collaborations to provide youth input into creating more effective nonprofit programming. To ensure youth input is specifically and consistently incorporated, *the Council calls for the expansion of an existing effort, or the creation of a new national youth council*, in addition to creating the Presidential Youth Working Group.
- Incorporate Youth Input Into Program Development and Evaluation. Nonprofit organizations (and foundations that support them) should *incorporate authentic youth input in the design and evaluation of programs and services for opportunity youth*. Specifically, nonprofits are encouraged to conduct constituency/beneficiary surveys of programs when assessing effectiveness and quality.

Youth as Leaders in the Solution:
Higher Attendance Rates

Voices of Youth in Chicago Education (VOYCE) is a youth-led collaborative for education justice. Since its formation in 2007, VOYCE has worked toward increasing Chicago's graduation rate by using youth-driven research and organizing to advance district-level policies that support student achievement.

To lay the foundation for VOYCE's campaign, more than 100 youth conducted an in-depth, year-long participatory action research project on the root causes of the city's 50 percent graduation rate. Based on this research, they launched a campaign to end the specific disciplinary measures that push students out of school and increase investment in student supports.

Student leaders successfully organized a pilot program aimed at increasing social-emotional supports for struggling freshmen, engaging more than 700 freshmen and 250 older peer mentors in peer mentoring, youth-led retreats, and personalized graduation planning. This pilot successfully impacted attitudes, relationships, and attendance rates. Partner schools have integrated these practices into their school-level programming, and VOYCE's campaign for safe and supportive schools has advanced to changing district-level policies that replace extreme disciplinary practices with research-based student supports, and prevention and intervention systems such as the initiative piloted by VOYCE.

White House Council for Community Solutions. *Case Studies of Effective Collaboratives.* 2011. http://www.serve.gov/new-images/ comm_collabs_ case_studies.pdf

2. **Create an Online, Youth-Rated Service Directory.** Social sector and faith-based leaders in every community should expand an existing or create a new community-wide service inventory, youth networking and/or customer feedback tool that youth can use to assess the quality and availability of local support services. We applaud http://www. FindYouthInfo.gov, and we encourage the administration to increase its efforts and challenge the nonprofit sector to *identify a third party to extend the reach of the information in http://www.FindYouthInfo.gov and to incorporate the ability for youth to rate and recommend listings.*

3. **Hire Opportunity Youth in Program Roles.** To create more relevant youth programs and reduce stigma mistakenly attached to opportunity youth, all programs that serve youth—government, business, nonprofit, faith-based, cross sector, etc.—should *assess which of their program and advocacy needs can be filled directly by the youth they aim to serve.* The Council suggests that the Interagency Working Group on Youth Programs may be appropriate to undertake this assessment for the federal government.

We believe implementation of these recommendations will dramatically improve the efficacy of programs serving opportunity youth.

> It's values, it's attitude, it's security, it's stability. All the things that young people, our own kids need, these kids need. And they're sitting here telling you what the outcomes could be if you give them a chance. If you provide them with the resources, they'll do the rest of the work.
>
> *– Bill Strickland*
> *Founder and CEO, Manchester Craftman's Guild*

Strategy Four: Build More Robust on-Ramps to Employment

Opportunity youth can be connected to employment successfully when multiple on-ramps linked to education and employment and designed to fit their community and youth needs are available and growing.

Because the needs of opportunity youth are diverse, it is necessary to meet them where they are by offering multiple on-ramps to employment—including education and service with job readiness training. Building on the Harvard Graduate School of Education's report *Pathways to Prosperity,* the PACE report *Civic Pathways Out of Poverty and Into Prosperity,* and Civic Enterprises' *Opportunity Road*, the Council's research pointed to opportunities to expand existing on-ramps and to build more robust on-ramps by increasing awareness of and access to wrap-around supports that will put youth on a path to reconnection.

The Council focused on three key engagement strategies that serve as on-ramps to employment for opportunity youth, listed below.

- **Direct to Employment**: Employers being actively engaged to successfully reconnect youth to employment through soft skills (e.g., communications, teamwork, time management) development, work-ready skills development, or learn and earn employment programs.
- **Relevant Education and Credentialing**: The education sector employing strategies to reconnect youth to education (secondary and postsecondary) and to help prevent disconnection through programs with accessibility and relevancy to opportunity youth needs.

- **Structured, Long-Term Service Programs**: Community and national service opportunities providing on-ramps for youth to gain work/life skills needed to reconnect to education and workforce opportunities.

The approach to reconnecting youth requires a multi-sector, all-in effort to be successful. It requires active engagement of different partners and is not a single actor with a single program. The interconnectedness of employers, education systems, and service—along with communities and nonprofits providing wrap-around supports—is critical for effective reconnection of this population. While the on-ramps are discussed separately, each is highly interconnected with the others, and all rely on a foundation of wrap-around support systems provided through organizations that serve youth.

Youth may need alternative learning models, soft or work-ready skills, flexible employment options, or overall integrated social support systems to enable them to take up opportunities. Employers, service organizations, educators, and youth service organizations can all play a role in meeting the needs of youth by collaborating in multi-sector efforts.

Direct to Employment

Youth unemployment is higher than for other age groups. Seventeen percent (unadjusted) of youth were out of work in February 2012, with less than half of youth employed. By contrast, the unemployment rate for those 25 and older was 7.4 percent, with 61 percent employed. And the 11 percent who never graduate or obtain a GED find it even harder to find employment. The unemployment rate for those adults was 14.8 percent, compared with 9.2 percent for high school graduates.

Additionally, the existing workforce does not match the job requirements of the future. Georgetown University's Center on Education and the Workforce predicts a skills gap of approximately three million postsecondary degrees and 4.7 million postsecondary certificates by 2018. Even today, 80 percent of manufacturers report they cannot find people to fill their skilled production jobs, translating to more than 500,000 unfilled manufacturing jobs; some 53 percent of large employers and 67 percent of small business leaders report they cannot find qualified nonmanagerial employees.

Benefits for Employers

Johns Hopkins Health System provides work readiness and job skills training to low-skilled, entry-level workers (and others interested) through courses taught at the hospital. Through reduction in employee turnover, the program has generated a 79 percent return on investment, and Hopkins can adjust the curriculum based on its needs.

Corporate Voices for Working Families. Building the Business Case for Investing in Tomorrow's Workforce: Employers See Positive Returns from Community Partnerships. 2011.

Based on research of successful employer programs for opportunity youth, the Council believes every employer can play a role in creating paths to employment. Approximately 50 percent of opportunity youth surveyed indicated that they do not have enough work experience to get the kind of job they want. Employers have a great deal to offer young people to better prepare them for work and equip them with the right skills, experience, and outlook. Whether providing work-relevant soft skills through one-on-one mentoring or workshops, hosting job shadow days, or providing youth with an opportunity to learn on the job and develop marketable skills while receiving compensation, employers can make a difference in creating opportunities to help youth get back on track.

In addition to the impact on the youth, there is a clear benefit to employers who thoughtfully develop programs for opportunity youth. Employers have reported increases in employee engagement, customer loyalty, and employee retention. These programs also provide employers with an improved local talent pipeline, help further diversity objectives, and contribute to the societal benefits of stronger communities as a whole.

Ways Employers Can Engage: The Three Lanes
Based on nationwide stakeholder listening sessions and extensive case study analysis of employers operating successful youth programs, the Council developed a set of best practices for employer engagement. These include establishing clear youth selection criteria, creating flexible education support, and providing on-the-job learning along with working with a nonprofit partner, setting high expectations, and ensuring wrap-around services are available. Building on this research, the Council identified three fundamental lanes of engagement through which a business can support youth: developing soft

skills; developing work-ready skills; and offering learn and earn employment opportunities.

Exhibit 4. Three Lanes of Employer Engagement

SOFT SKILLS DEVELOPMENT	WORK-READY SKILLS DEVELOPMENT	LEARN & EARN PROGRAMS
Opportunities that provide youth with work-relevant soft skills via course work and/or direct experience	Opportunities that provide youth with insight into the world of work to prepare them for employment	Opportunities for youth to develop on-the-job skills in a learning environment while receiving wages for their work
Examples: • Soft skills workshops • Employee mentors	Examples: • Job shadow days • Career exploration guidance • Job readiness training	Examples: • Paid internships with structured training and support (e.g., buddy) • Permanent positions with structured training and support (e.g., mentor)

Soft skills are critical to success in the workplace. Company employees with a few years or more of work experience can be insightful guides for opportunity youth through one-on-one mentorship, coaching sessions, and workshops. This type of support can range from medium- to long-term commitments (e.g., mentoring) to one-time events (e.g., workshops) and is the most flexible of the three lanes of engagement.

Soft Skills Program Highlight

Southwire, a manufacturer of cables and wires in Georgia, has employees work with the Carroll County schools as mentors for young students. This allows students to combine their studies with on-the-job training (and a paycheck) in its wire manufacturing plant.

Corporate Voices for Working Families. Building the Business Case for Investing in Tomorrow's Workforce: Employers See Positive Returns from Community Partnerships. 2011.

Experiencing the world of work close to the source, youth begin to have a better sense of what it takes to be ready for work. Employers can host job shadow days, offer career exploration guidance, and provide job readiness training. These types of **work-ready** skills programs can be sources of inspiration for a young person and can spark a focused interest in a field or area of study.

Work-Ready Skills Program Highlight

Gap Inc. created a program called This Way Ahead (delivered in partnership through a New York-based nonprofit, The Door) to expose opportunity youth to career exploration, job readiness training, internships, and follow-up support. In this program, 80 percent of employees improved their leadership skills as a result of volunteering.

Gap, Inc.; TCC Group, December 2009, *Evaluation Report for Gap Foundation's This Way Ahead Youth Program.* http://www. bewhatspossible.com/Home/TargetCauses.aspx

---

Learn and earn programs can provide opportunity youth with the best of both worlds: an opportunity to learn on the job and develop marketable skills, and an opportunity to receive compensation for their work. These programs can come in the form of internships, apprenticeships, and permanent positions, which are usually coupled with a mentor or buddy and structured training.

It is essential that employers engaging youth work closely with a nonprofit partner. Opportunity youth can have a range of challenges in their lives, and having a partner skilled in working directly with these young people can be of great value to a business. In addition to robust partnerships, measuring the results of company efforts to assess the value to the business and make the case for continuation or expansion of the program is critical.

Learn and Earn Program Highlight

CVS Caremark created regional learning centers to source, train, and hire entry-level workers. The program helps untapped talent enter the industry and progress along the career path by offering innovative training, career mentoring, and education encouragement. Since the program's inception, the company has doubled its retention rate and has generated a 179 percent return on investment (return relative to costs on Work Opportunity Tax Credit).

> CVS's research shows a 30 percent higher retention rate among employees from these learning centers.
>
> Corporate Voices for Working Families. *Learn and Earn Micro-Business Case Series*. 2011. http://www.corporatevoices.org/our-work/pse/ micro_cases

Key Recommendations

Encourage All Sectors to Increase Job Opportunities for Opportunity Youth

- The Council was honored to participate in the administration's Summer Jobs+ initiative that partnered with corporate leaders with a goal of providing 250,000 private, government, and nonprofit sector opportunities for disconnected and disadvantaged youth in the summer of 2012. We recommend the administration continue and deepen this initiative by *increasing the target for jobs and other opportunities as currently defined in Summer Jobs+ every year, encouraging the creation of more year-round opportunities in addition to summer jobs, and by expanding this initiative to include the faith-based community*. All employers should be made aware of the tools available in *Employer Tool Kit: Connecting Youth to Employment* and should be encouraged to include mutually beneficial youth employment programs as part of their corporate social responsibility strategy.
- We applaud the administration for pledging to hire more than 20,000 opportunity or disadvantaged youth through Summer Jobs+. We encourage the administration to continue and deepen this initiative by committing to increase the number of jobs each year and by providing year-round opportunities *in addition to annual summer opportunities*.
- We applaud the administration's support of the Disconnected Youth Opportunity Tax Credit, which was authorized in the American Recovery and Reinvestment Act of 2010 and provides a tax credit to employers who hire disadvantaged youth. We recommend that the administration, with the support of Congress, *continue to build on the Disconnected Youth Opportunity Tax Credit and to strengthen it by including incentives for employers to provide a range of valuable experiences from job shadowing, career awareness, mentoring or internship programs to hiring opportunity youth.*

Successful Programs Partner with Local Nonprofits

LinkedIn and Year Up work together to provide opportunities for opportunity youth. Year Up is a nonprofit organization that provides a year of training to help prepare urban young adults for career advancement and higher education opportunities. Students receive technical and professional skills, college credits, an educational stipend, and a six-month-long corporate internship with local partner companies. The program focuses on developing skills in several areas: IT/help desk support, investment operations, and quality assurance.

LinkedIn is one of the first Silicon Valley-based companies to participate as a corporate partner in Year Up's program. At LinkedIn, the interns performed rotations in the IT department. In June 2011 LinkedIn Director of Corporate IT Mike Jennings wrote, "We've been very impressed with the results that the interns have delivered during their time here. In addition to providing technical support for LinkedIn's employees, they've become a valuable part of our team, adding energy and enthusiasm while helping reduce our team's workload."

Relevant Education and Credentialing[8]

Opportunity youth often lack the credentials (high school diploma, GED, technical or postsecondary education) that lead to success in life. In fact, 47 percent of opportunity youth say they lack enough education to get their ideal job.[9] Additionally, many "best-in-class" programs are still inaccessible for the majority of opportunity youth because they require prerequisite academic skills that many of these young people lack. Youth often remain disconnected because the solutions offered by many well-meaning institutions and individuals are not tied to the systems the youth are disconnected from, or even to the issues they are facing.

Effective education efforts aimed at opportunity youth are comprehensive, youth-centered, flexible, and pragmatic. Successful interventions are those that encompass a multi-sector approach and link education to social services, mental health services, employment, and/or job training. The Council believes that educational efforts to prevent disconnection and innovative programs to encourage postsecondary reconnection and completion that follow these best practices can provide additional pathways for opportunity youth.

Education Solutions: Prevention

Strive, a nonprofit based in Cincinnati, has brought together more than 300 local leaders from the private, government, secondary, and postsecondary education and nonprofit sectors to drive educational progress through collective impact, resource alignment, and data-informed decision-making. Stakeholders co-developed a common agenda, evaluation standards, and a consistent communication platform with the vision of improving the education system throughout greater Cincinnati and northern Kentucky. Strive's goals directly relate to the prevention of disconnected youth by preparing every child for school; supporting children inside and outside of school; promoting academic success; and aiming to ensure that every child enrolls and succeeds in some form of postsecondary education.

Stakeholders who participate in Strive share a common agenda, but their individual activities are not uniform. Instead, participants perform coordinated activities at which they excel and which support Strive's overarching mission. All activities are informed by the shared metrics. In the four years since its inception, the program has achieved impressive successes. Stakeholders set aside their individual agendas in favor of a collective approach in order to solve this entrenched, systemic problem.

White House Council for Community Solutions. *Case Studies of Effective Collaboratives.* 2011. http://www.serve.gov/ new-images/council/pdf/comm collabs case studies.pdf

---

Keeping Youth Engaged in Education

A student's decision to drop out of school is not the result of a single life event. To the contrary, issues such as poor attendance, behavior, and problems with course completion begin to manifest as early as elementary school and into middle school. Emerging proactive strategies that address dropouts focus on students in elementary and middle schools. But early identification of students at risk of disconnection is only a first step. The key to preventing disconnection is developing the capacity of public education to mitigate the risk factors and help students stay connected, graduate, and be prepared for college and careers. Communities must develop a collective commitment and belief that graduation rates can improve through the early, data-driven identification of potentially disconnected students, the application of diverse multi-sector strategies to address student needs, and a public education system with the capacity to provide them.

Re-engaging Opportunity Youth in Education

Innovative secondary programs, as well as postsecondary institutions, can be critical in re-engaging youth in education. Alternative GED programs and charter schools that allow for internships or other work connections are examples of how secondary education programs can be more engaging for opportunity youth.

Increasingly, colleges and universities across the nation—many of which are anchor institutions in their communities—are getting more involved in their communities and interested in the topic of youth development and alternative education. By virtue of their missions, community colleges are uniquely positioned to provide pathways to success for opportunity youth. The federal government's emphasis on and support of community colleges has the potential to provide many more opportunities for youth. Community colleges can play a critical role in re-engaging opportunity youth by providing programs for remediation and career-oriented, competency-based instruction. When they partner with other leaders from the educational and social sectors, community colleges have even greater potential to positively impact at-risk youth.

Educational Solutions: Youth Re-Engagement

The Gateway to College program allows high school dropouts to enroll in community colleges across the country to gain the competencies needed to graduate from high school while accumulating credits toward a postsecondary credential. This program, originating at the Portland Community College in Portland, Oregon, has been replicated at 29 colleges in 16 states. Students in the Gateway to College program attend classes on the college campus; they are college students. The program pays the cost of admission, fees, and books. Gateway to College uses public education funding and the college infrastructure to support the program.

In addition to providing academic support, Gateway to College offers wrap-around services to address the social and emotional needs of students. Students are provided an opportunity to learn within a small cadre of their peers and are taught by a team of instructors and resource specialists.

After the first year of intensive transitional guidance to build their academic and personal skills, students join the general college student population. The program combines high expectations with personal coaching and support.

Although the Gateway to College program is relatively new, early data indicate promising results. Students who experienced poor attendance rates in high school show an increase in attendance at Gateway to College (an average rate of 82 percent.) To date, Gateway to College students have passed 72 percent of nearly 70,000 college courses with a C or better.

White House Council for Community Solutions. *Case Studies of Effective Collaboratives.* 2011. http://www. serve.gov/new-images/council/pdf /comm_collabs_ case_studies.pdf

Bridging the Gap between Education and Employment

One innovative type of educational program, a bridge program, is designed to create comprehensive pathways for youth to and through postsecondary programs and/or employment opportunities, bridging the students' experience from high school to postsecondary education or from postsecondary education to employment.

Successful bridge programs incorporate strategic partnerships with education leaders at the secondary and postsecondary levels, as well as the employment and social sectors. Such partnerships allow students to access bridge programs through a variety of avenues, gain knowledge and experience that is relevant to their career aspirations, and receive guidance on a range of topics and issues.

Educational Solutions: Partnering With Employers

In a new study by the Manufacturing Institute (http://www. themanufacturinginstitute.org/Research/Skills-Gap-inManufacturing/2011- Skills-Gap-Report/2011-Skills-Gap-Report.aspx) more than 80 percent of manufacturers report they cannot find people to fill their skilled production jobs. As a result, more than 500,000 manufacturing jobs are open right now. Responding to this talent crisis and to the need to create jobs in this country, the Institute worked with the President's Jobs Council to tailor the national manufacturing certification system into a nationally replicable fast-track solution to deliver just in time talent to small manufacturers.

This accelerated program, Right Skills Now, allows individuals to earn college credit and national industry certifications in 16 weeks, preparing them for immediate employment in high-quality manufacturing jobs and giving them a solid foundation to advance in higher education and careers.

In addition, these types of innovative partnerships between education and employment are critical to ensuring our youth get the type of skills our labor market is demanding.

This multi-sector approach can help youth reconnect and prepare for the workforce, while equipping them with the most relevant set of skills.

Educational Solutions: Community Colleges Connecting Education to Employment

Skills for America's Future is an initiative of the Aspen Institute to create a national network of partnerships among employers, community colleges, industry associations, and other stakeholders. These partnerships are designed to ensure Americans receive the training necessary to meet the needs of employers and have the opportunity to get and keep good jobs. Since the initiative was announced in October 2010, Skills for America's Future has successfully helped create or expand partnerships between more than 30 employers and 200 community colleges across the country.

An example is Metropolitan College, a Louisville, Kentucky-based partnership between UPS, government, and postsecondary educational institutions. The program offers participants both financial support for study and part-time employment at UPS.

As of 2010, 2,600 individuals, who had participated in Metropolitan College for one or more semesters, had earned 3,760 credentials including 1,024 certificates, 966 associate's degrees, 1,576 bachelor's degrees, and 194 advanced degrees.

In addition to benefits for participants, Metropolitan College has dramatically stabilized UPS's overnight workforce and provided reliable, skilled employees to staff UPS operations in Louisville.

Key Recommendations

Provide   High-Quality,   Relevant   Educational   Opportunities   for Opportunity Youth

- *We applaud the administration's Blueprint for Investing in America's Future: Transforming Career and Technical Education* (GTE) and in particular its four core principles: alignment, collaboration, accountability, and innovation. The administration's proposal would use a combination of technical assistance, competition, and a system of structured rewards to ensure that more students, regardless of backgrounds or circumstances, have access to high-quality GTE programs. The current act provides separate funding streams for local education agencies and postsecondary institutions, making alignment challenging, and weakening a student's ability to transition between secondary and postsecondary systems. The administration's proposal would discontinue this approach by requiring states to competitively fund consortia of Local Education Agencies (LEAs), postsecondary institutions, and their partners. The proposal includes provisions to ensure competitive funding has no adverse impact on access for vulnerable student populations including, for instance, the authority for states to establish absolute funding priorities. The proposal would also require that at least one of the LEAs in the consortia serve a high concentration of students from low-income families and allow resources for states to provide services for opportunity youth.

- We applaud the Department of Education's Together for Tomorrow initiative to involve faith-based and other community organizations in developing and supporting programs that increase school attendance, improve behavior, support academic achievement, and increase college accessibility. We recommend the administration encourage the postsecondary education community to *scale effective examples of community- and faith-based organizations to provide opportunity youth the remediation, support services, and career-oriented instruction necessary for their success.*

- The administration should *encourage the K-12 system to do more data-driven early identification and prevention of school disconnection.* Specifically, early warning information and intervention systems should be put in place in schools to identify those students whose attendance, behavior, and course completion records signal the need for school-based and community-based supports. These systems should be combined with appropriate programs for recovery.

- Encourage school districts and community and faith-based organizations to provide high-quality remedial and dropout recovery services to opportunity youth. Gurrent offerings are not sufficient to meet the need. Regulations should *encourage dropout recovery services, and Race to the Top should include selection criteria for applicants including reconnecting opportunity youth strategies in their state plans.*

- We applaud the administration's support of Skills for America's Future, an industry-led initiative to improve industry partnerships with community colleges and build a nationwide network to maximize workforce development strategies, job training programs, and job placements. We recommend that the administration *continue its support of efforts that meet the needs of local employers in today's dynamic economy.*

- We recommend the administration encourage the military and employers to work closely with higher education institutions to align work experience with curriculum for degree-granting programs to allow those participating in qualifying military and employer training or work experiences to earn academic credit.

Structured, Long-Term Service Programs

A structured, long-term service program is a viable path for opportunity youth to connect to postsecondary education and the workforce. In fact, nearly seven in ten (69 percent) of opportunity youth surveyed want to make a difference in the lives of others, while only three percent report that they are volunteering. This indicates that there is an untapped interest in service opportunities, and these very opportunities can provide a path to further education and employment. In fact, service has long been an on-ramp to the nonprofit field, which is one of the fastest growing occupations in our economy today.

Existing Service Programs Offer Opportunity for Youth

The roots of the modern service movement took hold during the Great Depression of the 1930s when the Civilian Conservation Corps put three million young people to work over a decade to restore the nation's parks and developing infrastructure, while allowing those young people to support themselves and their families. Today there are many opportunities for service both locally and nationally. Full-time, structured, long-term (at least six months) service programs for youth can provide a meaningful transition to either employment or education. Participants do real work helping communities address issues in education, health, poverty, housing, conservation, veterans' services, and disaster preparedness and relief.

These service programs often include program elements recognized as best practices in successfully engaging youth, including high expectations, wrap-around support, work-relevant learning opportunities, and a connected, caring adult.

Service: Connecting Opportunity Youth to Education

Support for educational achievement that service programs provide is an incentive to enroll in a service program. Such programs are also often transformational in the lives of opportunity youth. The primary educational support offered by many such service programs is the Segal AmeriCorps Education Award that is given upon completion of service and can be applied to further postsecondary expenses or to repay qualified student loans.

Service as a Path to Education

AmeriCorps National Civilian Community Corps (NCCC) partnered with the Nonprofit Leadership Alliance to create a nonprofit leadership certificate. A member's experience earns them most of the requirements for the certificate program, including fulfilling the internship requirement. AmeriCorps NCCC works closely with partner universities to enroll students in the remaining required courses. The Louisiana State University in Shreveport, for example, offers NCCC additional benefits like waiving the GRE requirement, allowing members to pay in-state tuition, and providing the option to take classes online. Graduates of NCCC also earn an educational award to apply toward future post-secondary courses.

Additionally, many service programs have a built-in academic curriculum and offer other external educational opportunities. Remedial and GED-prep courses are offered in many programs. Others offer courses in specific industries to allow members to earn nationally recognized certifications.

Service programs are taking additional steps to improve their members' educational outcomes. Some service programs are now holding education fairs, building postsecondary partnerships, including setting up college credit agreements in which participants receive undergraduate credit for completing their service programs, and providing online transition guidance for service members completing their terms.

Service: Connecting Opportunity Youth to Employment

In addition to encouraging educational aspirations of members, many service programs have workforce development initiatives that equip youth with essential skills they need to be contributing members in the economy and their communities. Graduates of service programs enhance their employability through acquisition of various soft skills and work-ready skills developed through specifically designed program elements geared toward enhanced employability, and a new social network.

Service As a Path to Employment

Through the National Guard Youth ChalleNGe Program, cadets have the opportunity to develop work-ready skills through career assessment and interest inventories, job-specific skills orientation and awareness, and training in area vocational centers. Classes cover the development of individual resumes, how to complete job applications, and what is needed to prepare for and go through a job interview. Key to success is a self-selected mentor that works with the cadet to develop a 12-month post-residential plan to help guide them after graduation. The mentor remains in contact for a full year after the cadet has completed the program, ensuring that the life plan is being followed.

Service programs are an especially effective pipeline for jobs in the fast-growing nonprofit sector. The nonprofit sector employs 10.5 million workers or one-tenth of all U.S. workers. It is the third largest industry behind manufacturing and retail. From 2008 to 2010, while private sector employment declined eight percent, nonprofit employment grew 4.5 percent. Because many opportunity youth have been clients of nonprofit services, their experience makes them especially prepared to be service providers and leaders on issues they know well.

Skills training is inherent in the nature of service programs. Whether it is work-ready skills such as CPR training, disaster relief, construction or health care, service programs require on-the-job training as part of the experience and many require pre-service training as well. Members also develop soft skills such as a strong work ethic, time management skills, respect for authority, self-advocacy, leadership, public speaking, flexibility, resourcefulness, and teamwork.

Furthermore, many service programs connect their members to opportunities that help their graduates transition into the workplace. Some programs conduct workshops on building resumes, teach business etiquette or provide mentors to help members develop "life plans." Mock interview sessions are also available in some programs.

These new skills translate to employment opportunities. According to a 2008 independent report, AmeriCorps VISTA members were consistently more likely to be employed than their counterparts in the comparison group. Despite similarities in career choices, VISTA members reported a higher current income profile than their counterparts in the comparison group.[10] Additionally, 67 percent of AmeriCorps state and national members and 70 percent of AmeriCorps NCCC members report that their experiences provided them with an advantage in finding a job.[11]

History has proven and programs today show evidence that service can provide a viable path for opportunity youth to education and employment. While many programs are successful today, the Council believes that it will require the service sector working more closely with the educational and employment sectors to improve and expand these on-ramps for opportunity youth.

> And through the love and respect of both of those (national service) programs, we were allowed to utilize that energy, and channel that into something that became community outreach, things that build our communities, make better leaders, and also helped in our situations.
>
> – Kareema Barr
> Youth Build Graduate

Key Recommendations

1. Increase Service Opportunities Available to Opportunity Youth and Ensure Strong Links to Education and Employment
   - We applaud AmeriCorps National Civilian Community Corps' (NCCC) 50 percent target for disadvantaged youth members and the new Federal Emergency Management Agency/NCCC initiative that

creates more service opportunities for opportunity youth. We recommend Corporation for National and Community Service (CNCS) *expand this effort by setting annual targets to increase the percentage of disadvantaged youth slots available and by establishing a cross-cutting priority for all programs that engage opportunity youth in service*, to ensure that its impact priorities do not disadvantage programs that engage such young people. Grant-based service programs should provide incentives through rewarding programs that propose and show evidence of successfully serving opportunity youth.

- Many service programs have established evidence of success in providing an on-ramp for youth from service to education and employment. Many of these same service programs also have waiting lists. The Council *recommends that the administration support and Congressional leaders, state and local governments respond by scaling successful evidence-based service programs.*

- We applaud the inclusion of the Opportunity Corps in the Edward M. Kennedy Serve America Act. The Council recommends implementing this initiative to reconnect youth and enlist their help in boosting the social mobility of others in their communities.

- We applaud the progress being made by the 21st Century Corps Initiative in creating stronger links between corps service and successful careers. CNCS should *continue to promote stronger links to education and employment,* including elements from transition to work programs such as providing academic credits from educational institutions and certifications from training programs and focusing on critical workforce skills that can be developed through service.

2. Help Opportunity Youth Find Mentors

- We applaud the administration's mentoring efforts including the First Lady's Corporate Mentoring Challenge and the Office of Juvenile Justice and Delinquency Prevention's multiple mentoring initiatives and *recommend that these efforts be expanded and deepened by encouraging youth-initiated mentoring.*

CLOSING SUMMARY

Community collaboratives with specific key attributes can achieve significant improvement in a variety of persistent community issues. While a dozen of these successful collaboratives were documented through the Council's research, approximately 100 more were identified as moving in the direction of accomplishing needle-moving change. With the right tools and supports, these promising collaboratives are poised to create significant improvement in their communities.

The population of opportunity youth is large and eager to take charge of their futures, but at the same time, it has complex and diverse needs. The benefits of reconnecting these youth to education or employment are enormous and require urgent action from all sectors.

Many efforts are expanding or being initiated to drive the growth of both successful community collaboratives and solutions for opportunity youth, including the Office of Management and Budget Performance Partnership Pilots, the United Way Community Conversations, and a new Aspen Institute Forum for Community Solutions. (Please see Appendix C for more examples of new efforts under way.)

With evidence in hand and movement underfoot, the Council believes that implementing the recommendations highlighted in this report—driving the development of successful cross-sector community collaboratives, creating a nationwide awareness and accountability for opportunity youth, engaging youth as leaders in the solution, and building more robust on-ramps to employment—will lead to significant progress on solving many persistent community issues, including ensuring all of our young people are on the path to prosperity.

APPENDIX A: STAKEHOLDER OUTREACH SUMMARY

Background

Members of the White House Council for Community Solutions engaged diverse stakeholders from across the country in meetings, roundtables, community-based listening sessions, and webinars between the months of March and May 2011. Formal listening sessions were held in New Orleans, Louisiana; Atlanta, Georgia; Houston, Texas; San Francisco, California; and Cincinnati, Ohio. This document provides a synthesis of the input collected from the more than 300 stakeholders across communities and sectors.

Key Findings: What Young People Need to Reconnect and Succeed

Programs

- Holistic programs, or network of services, that address a full range of needs, with additional "seats" (capacity) in existing programs that work (rather than accessing multiple programs to meet each specific need)
- Accessible programs that are personalized and include a caring adult (mentor) and the opportunity to build social networks
- Multiple paths to success, including a variety of on-ramps and reentry paths that meet young people where they are
- Effective programs that address the needs of those youth performing significantly below grade level when they leave the education system (estimated to be up to 70 percent of opportunity youth)
- High-quality, relevant education and job training programs that prepare youth for real job opportunities and better access to relevant work experience

Communication

- Expanded outreach to increase young peoples' awareness of programs that work
- Elimination of stereotypes of the limitations of opportunity youth and messaging that reinforces youth as assets

Prevention and Intervention

- Improvements to systems that fail youth and lead to the point of disconnection (e.g., foster care, education, juvenile justice)
- Involvement of caring adults, (including parents and guardians, when possible) to be mentors and positive role models
- Opportunities for positive peer support

Key Findings: What's Needed for Effective Cross-Sector Collaboration

- Clearly defined problem, trust among stakeholders, community-wide common goals and metrics and data-driven decisions

- Effective design involving all stakeholders, e.g., youth, educators, employers, credentialing entities, youth-serving organizations, and other stakeholders
- Incentives for existing collaboratives to address challenges facing youth rather than formation of new collaboratives

Key Findings: What Stakeholders Need to Move Forward

- A common language articulating the challenge, a clearly defined business case for each stakeholder, and proof that transformation is possible
- Defined opportunities to engage and add value that align with stakeholders' missions and capitalize on organizational competencies
- Better access to and alignment of public (state/local/federal) and private resources
- Engagement of noncorporate employers (e.g., local government, universities, health care, among others), particularly those with growth in job opportunities

APPENDIX B: UNITED WAY OPPORTUNITY COMMUNITY CONVERSATIONS

Background

United Way Worldwide planned a series of Opportunity Community Conversations to bring together people, businesses, government, and nonprofits to create real change in education, income, and health. In response to President Obama's call to action at the January 5, 2012, Summer Jobs + event, United Way Worldwide invited the Council to participate in these conversations throughout the country. This resulted in more than 125 community conversations occurring from February through March 2012.

The community conversations were hosted and managed on a voluntary basis by the local United Way affiliates, with leadership and support from United Way Worldwide. Each affiliate that participated committed to holding three to five conversations. Many of these conversations were with everyday people, and at least one conversation in each community included community leaders.

Summary

Across the nation, community conversations including youth, families, adults, community, nonprofit, business, and government leaders surfaced common challenges and opportunities for addressing the needs of opportunity youth. In describing their toughest challenges, youth reported difficulty navigating and accessing local services, a dearth of mentors and role models, inadequate pathways to meaningful employment and education, and a concern for basic safety. Across communities, youth were characterized by a distrust of government, preferring to engage with local organizations. A strong entrepreneurial spirit also characterized youth, with many calling for a louder voice and a more prominent role in serving their local communities. Youth are coping with common struggles: many expressed frustration with their family unit, disillusionment with local schools and law enforcement, and disenchantment with the lack of employment opportunities tailored specifically for youth.

These findings point to great opportunity for improvement, including more collaboration between service providers, more mentors, a more individualized approach to services for youth, youth involvement in creating solutions, and greater accessibility to information about available services.

Overview of Community Conversations

The Council participated in the community conversations to meet three objectives:

- To spark informed action in communities around the nation, creating solutions for disconnected youth.
- To make sure that information about opportunity youth and the tools for addressing their needs were disseminated widely to those who are in the best position to create opportunities for these youth.
- To inform the recommendations in the Council's final report to the President by gathering information on what works and on the challenges and opportunities in implementing community solutions.

The United Way affiliates invited attendees based on their network in their local communities. In addition, Council members worked with affiliates to create a mix of participants who are thought leaders and innovators in the area of collaborative efforts and opportunity youth.

The moderated discussions were framed with data from two research reports *Opportunity Road: The Promise and Challenges of America's Forgotten Youth* and *The Economic Value of Opportunity Youth*.

The discussion engaged participants in an in-depth dialogue around the following topics:

- What creates opportunities/a good life in a community?
- What is standing in the way of achieving this opportunity?
- What could be done to create these opportunities/good lives?
- Specifically with regard to opportunity youth:
  - What successful programs exist?
  - Who should be at the table to create opportunities, and what would it take to get them involved?
  - What challenges and opportunities exist in this community in addressing the needs of opportunity youth?

Key Findings

Youth Aspirations

Across cities and conversations, in discussing aspirations, responses are strongly consistent. First and foremost, youth want safety, a palpable sense of community engagement, a strong family unit, and a credible opportunity to realize the American dream. Youth want to live in an environment that is safe, inclusive of diversity (including differences in sexual orientation and identity), and supportive of youth and their aspirations. Along these lines, youth want to live in neighborhoods in which neighbors and community members are explicitly positive and supportive, not actively destructive or pessimistic. Youth want to enjoy an educational system that prepares them for a better future. Youth want access to meaningful employment. Critical to meaningful employment and to enjoying a meaningful future more broadly is mentorship. Youth want access to quality mentorship and exemplary role models because youth want to feel supported day-to-day and youth recognize how important mentorship is in successfully navigating an increasingly complex job and educational market.

Interestingly, a common aspiration among youth is also a strong desire to be free of government intervention and support. There is a powerful aversion to dependence on government that emerges in the conversations. However, youth consistently held high hopes for their communities and, oftentimes, respected the community organizations striving to serve them. Importantly, youth aspire to be helped by their communities, not government.

Lastly, youth aspire to serve their communities, too. Youth aspire to have a louder voice in their communities and want to play a stronger role in confronting common challenges. Youth are extremely entrepreneurial, but have few means available to them through which to exercise their pioneering spirit. While youth certainly need support and services, youth also require an opportunity to serve and to give back.

Youth Challenges

Across the nation, youth most commonly identified the following as their most difficult challenges:

- Difficulty navigating and accessing local services. Accessing and navigating services is a challenge common among youth. Youth label services delivered by both the social sector and the government as fragmented, uncoordinated, insensitive to individual concerns, and stigmatizing. Youth are calling for services that are less stigmatizing, more individualized, and tightly integrated among providers.
- A dearth of role models and mentors. Youth are calling for more role models and mentors to help them with the difficult and often complex paths to rewarding employment and education. Traditional sources of mentorship have proven inadequate; youth are often disenchanted with local teachers, law enforcement, and even the family unit.
- Inadequate pathways to employment and education. The devastated economy and an increasingly competitive but deeply inadequate school system have taken a huge toll on youth and their prospects for opportunities. For many youth, there are few, if any, clear paths to meaningful employment or education. Youth need stronger on-ramps to paths leading to meaningful employment or education, and more guidance (e.g., mentorship) as they walk along these paths.
- Safety. A palpable sense of insecurity and danger is evident in many conversations with youth. This is compounded by the difficult relationship many youth have with local enforcement. Strengthening the relationship between youth, local law enforcement, and local

government could contribute to a greater sense of well-being among youth in their communities.

What Needs to Change?

Youth are asking for basic physical and economic security and educational and occupational opportunity. While there are organizations working to provide these things for youth, a frequent and passionate theme among adult participants was the frequency with which nonprofit and community organizations failed to coordinate, pool resources, and collaborate. Many of the adult participants cite the lack of connections among/between organizations and the negative effect that has on services to youth. Some organizations have reported creating databases of resources and referrals geared toward helping program participants. But organizations must go further.

Therefore, the prevalence of destructive turf wars was cited as a persistent theme. Many participants strongly desired a lead agency that acts as a neutral agent responsible for convening local parties; a good lead agency isn't necessarily a lead but rather a starting point for community change. Without collaboration, many youth are excluded from community services.

Youth were consistently emphatic about the need for role models and positive mentors. Simply, youth are not exposed to enough positive role models in their communities, nor are they receiving the individualized support that comes from having a mentor. Mentors are crucial to ensuring a meaningful work experience, to navigating the complex systems of public education as well as the difficulties inherent to many underserved communities.

Opportunities and Potential Recommendations

A number of possible recommendations emerged:

- Participants are calling for more collaboration among organizations to close critical gaps in services.
- Youth are calling for more role models and mentors.
- Participants are calling for organizations that effectively meet their individual needs and concerns.

- Youth are eager to be part of the solution; calls for more tutoring or peer counseling are common. However, youth report that they are rarely asked to serve their peers in their community.
- Adult participants are eager for a forum through which to better understand stakeholder concerns. Adults are often unclear as to the true needs of youth and often have no mechanism by which to surface those needs; moreover, adults are also unclear as to the mission and agenda of other organizations, and how to foster compelling collaboration.

APPENDIX C: EXAMPLES OF NEW EFFORTS UNDER WAY

The Council deeply appreciates the over 300 individuals and organizations that took the time to share their insights and ideas. Their counsel greatly influenced the Council's work and strengthened the recommendations in this report. The Council commends their continued commitment to supporting opportunity youth achieve their dreams.

The Council would like to acknowledge the following new efforts on behalf of opportunity youth. This list is not intended to be all-inclusive, given that many more efforts are under way or will be launched in the future.

Drive the Development of Successful Cross-Sector Community Collaborations

Aspen Forum for Community Solutions
The Aspen Institute is creating the Aspen Forum for Community Solutions, to be led by Melody Barnes, former assistant to the president and director of the Domestic Policy Council for President Obama, along with a senior-level executive director to drive and manage the day-to-day work. The forum will spotlight success stories, educate national and local leaders about this strategy, and provide community leaders with some of the knowledge and tools they will need to launch a successful collaborative.

The forum will focus on three key objectives:

- Engage and enlist community leaders to pull together for change.
- Provide the knowledge and tools communities need to create effective collaboratives.

- Incent more needle-moving community collaborations focused on opportunity youth through an opportunity youth incentive fund.

Reconnecting Opportunity Youth - Tulane University

In March 2012, the Cowen Institute for Public Education Initiatives at Tulane University launched its initiative Reconnecting Opportunity Youth. With funding support from AT&T, the Cowen Institute is examining the challenges that opportunity youth face, assessing services that are available to them currently in the Greater New Orleans area, and analyzing strategies that enable struggling youth to reach their potential and contribute to their community. Additionally, the institute is taking its findings and developing a specific community action plan to address the issue of opportunity youth in New Orleans—with the goal of creating an infrastructure of effective, sustainable, and meaningful services and programs that will prepare these young people for college and career. By sharing outcomes with the community and reaching out to key players, the Cowen Institute is laying the groundwork for collective impact. Following its call to action, the institute will initiate a citywide, multi-sector collaborative to accomplish systemic change and significantly increase the number of young New Orleanians who embark on paths that lead to careers and engaged lives.

United Way Opportunity Community Conversations and Common Good Awards

United Way Worldwide planned a series of Opportunity Community Conversations to bring together people, businesses, government, and nonprofits to create real change in education, income, and health. This resulted in more than 125 Community Conversations occurring from February through March 2012. These conversations are serving as the springboard for community-based action including new partnerships and jobs initiatives.

Additionally, United Way Worldwide launched a new effort to recognize collaboratives and partnerships that are advancing education, income, and health. The awards highlight innovative and promising practices from communities around the world that are making measurable progress in education, income and health—the building blocks for a good quality of life.

There were three overall award winners announced at the United Way Town Hall in May: The United Way Common Good Award for Advancing Education, Advancing Income, and Advancing Health. Winning community collaboratives each demonstrate a shared understanding of their community's challenges and a commitment to taking a joint approach to addressing them.

Family Independence Initiative Awards

The new Family Independence Initiative (FII) Award will recognize and reward groups of families, friends, and community members who have taken it upon themselves to organize and create solutions to engage and reconnect their youth to the larger community. As examples of how all communities are full of families with ideas, wisdom, and determination, honorees will inspire others to organize in their own communities.

There are numerous excellent programs that exist for young people, but often the most productive engagement for youth is with their families and friends in their communities. These everyday heroes don't work through an organization or agency; they do it on their own. They do it without the support of programs, services, or philanthropic funding. The FII Award will provide seed funding over two years to recognize four self-organized groups each year. It will also provide a venue for sharing with the nation that the seeds of change exist in our most disenfranchised communities.

Opportunity Nation Initiatives

Opportunity Nation (ON) is working along three key avenues to ensure ongoing progress for opportunity youth. ON will be hosting a revised and updated interactive version of *Employer Tool Kit: Connecting Youth to Employment*, as well as the *Community Collaboratives Tool Box*. It is working with Columbia University to ensure that the national data from *The Economic Value of Disconnected Youth* will be available on a community level. ON is also creating a plan of action for both public and private sectors to reach at least one million opportunity youth with efforts to reconnect them to education and employment.

Opportunity Nation is a broad coalition of nearly 200 businesses, nonprofits, educational institutions, and military organizations seeking to create a shared, bipartisan plan to create better skills, better jobs, and better communities.

Engage Youth As Leaders in the Solution

The Sparkopportunity Challenge

The SparkOpportunity Challenge is an initiative of SparkAction in partnership with the Youth Leadership Institute and dozens of leading youth-engagement organizations across the country. During the spring of 2012, young people were encouraged to propose their own visionary yet viable solutions to create jobs, build and enhance skills, and bring about real change for opportunity youth. The approaches to create local jobs generated through this challenge have the potential to be replicated in other communities.

Participants were instructed to upload a short video and/or text description of their ideas to SparkAction's contest platform. Winners to be announced in June 2012, will receive seed grants and technology to support starting their project up, and other opportunities, such as the chance to share their ideas with CEOs, government officials, and business leaders, and to receive feedback and assistance with implementation, a promotional video featuring their ideas, and help with fund-raising. (Winners will be listed on the Challenge web site, http://sparkaction.org/ sparkopportunity.)

The goal of the six-week challenge is to identify viable youth-driven solutions and to highlight the ideas and perspectives of young people. In the longer term, the challenge presents an opportunity to implement the winning ideas in communities around the country, potentially informing national strategies to improve the workforce and economy.

Youth Leadership Institute Youth Ambassadors

Over the past few months, the Youth Leadership Institute has recruited and trained 11 "youth ambassadors" to raise awareness and spark action on behalf of opportunity youth by serving as spokespeople in local and national forums.

The youth and young adults were selected because of their powerful personal stories about overcoming challenges to successfully engage in education and work, many of them through vital pathways that provided them with real work skills, mentors, internships, and social and financial support.

The Youth Leadership Institute created the Youth Ambassador Program as part of its effort to help bring powerful youth voices to national and community discussions inspired by the work of the White House Council for Community Solutions.

Build More Robust on-Ramps to Employment

Summer Jobs+

Summer Jobs+ is a call to action for businesses, nonprofits, and government to work together to provide pathways to employment for low-income and disconnected youth in the summer of 2012. As of May 2012, this initiative is providing nearly 300,000 opportunities. Employment opportunities include 90,000 paid jobs and thousands of mentorships, internships, and other training opportunities. This initiative is also launching the Summer Jobs+ Bank, a new online search tool to help connect young people to jobs, internships, and other employment opportunities this summer and year-round.

San Francisco Summer Jobs+ Launch

Inspired by the Department of Labor's Summer Jobs+ program, San Francisco Mayor Ed Lee and United Way of the Bay Area announced the launch of San Francisco Summer Jobs+ in April 2012. The initiative aims to create 5,000 jobs and paid internships for young people this summer. It is San Francisco's local response to President Obama's national call to action for businesses, nonprofits, and government to provide pathways to employment for young people, especially low-income and disconnected youth.

A local youth employment program, MatchBridge, will take the lead in the program to support young job seekers with resources such as work-readiness workshops, resume writing assistance, interview tips, and job-search coaching. MatchBridge will also work with employers to ensure a good match with youth employees.

APPENDIX D: BIBLIOGRAPHY

American Youth Policy Forum (2011). Key Considerations for Serving Disconnected Youth.

Ashby, Cornelia M. (2008). Disconnected Youth: Federal Action Could Address Some of the Challenges Faced by Local Programs That Reconnect Youth to Education and Employment. Washington, DC: United States Government Accountability Office.

Bauldry, Shawn, and Tracey A. Hartmann (2004). The Promise and Challenge of Mentoring High-Risk Youth: Findings from the National Faith-Based Initiative. Philadelphia: Private/Public Ventures. (2004).

Bernstein, Lawrence, Catherine Dun Rappaport, Lauren Olsho, Dana Hunt, Marjorie Levin (2009). Impact Evaluation of the US Department of Education's Student Mentoring Program. Washington, DC: Institute of Education Sciences.

Bloom, Dan, Saskia Levy Thompson, and Rob Ivry (2010). Building a Learning Agenda Around Disconnected Youth. New York: MDRC.

Boisi, Geoffrey T., Haim Saban, Alan D. Schwartz, and Gail Manza (2006). The National Agenda for Action: How to Close the Mentoring Gap. Alexandria, VA: MENTOR.

Bozell, Maureen R., and Melissa Goldberg (2009). Employers, Low-Income Young Adults, and Postsecondary Education Credentials: A Practical Typology for Business, Education, and Community Leaders. Barrington, RI: Workforce Strategy Center.

Bridgeland, John M., John J. DiIulio, Jr., and Karen Burke Morrison (2006). The Silent Epidemic: Perspectives of High School Drop-Outs. Washington, DC: Civic Enterprises.

Bridgeland, John M., Jessica Milano, and Elyse Rosenblum (2011). Across the Great Divide: Perspectives of CEOs and College Presidents on America's Higher Education and Skills Gap. Washington, DC: Civic Enterprises.

Brown Lerner, J., and Betsy Brand (2006). The College Ladder: Linking Secondary and Postsecondary Education for Success for All Students. Washington, DC: American Youth Policy Forum.

Campaign for Youth (2008). Our Youth, Our Economy, Our Future: A National Investment Strategy for Reconnecting America's Youth.

Campbell-Kibler Associates (2009). Youth Development Institute: Community Education Pathways to Success, Final Evaluation Report.

Carnevale, Anthony P., Nicole Smith, and Jeff Strohl (2010). Help Wanted: Projections for Jobs and Education Requirements through 2018. Washington, DC: Georgetown University Center on Education and the Workforce.

Carnavale, Anthony P., and Stephen J. Rose (2010). The Undereducated American. Washington, DC: Georgetown University Center on Education and the Workforce.

Corporate Voices for Working Families (2007). Business Leadership: Supporting Youth Development and the Talent Pipeline.

Corporation for National and Community Service (2006). AmeriCorps NCCC Fact Sheet.

Corporation for National and Community Service (2008). Nonprofit CEOs Hail AmeriCorps as Source for Future Leaders, Press Release.

Communities Collaborating to Reconnect Youth (2010). Recommitting to Our Nation's Youth: Building on the Legacy of Youth Opportunity Implications for Federal Policy.

Decision Information Resources (2007). Youth Opportunity Grants Initiative: Impact and Synthesis Report.

Decision Information Resources (2007). Youth Opportunity Grants Initiative: Management Information Systems Report – Revised Final.

Decision Information Resources (2007). Youth Opportunity Grant Initiative: Process Evaluation Final Report.

Dubois, David L. (2006). Youth Mentoring: Programs and Practices that Work, Forum Brief. Washington, DC: American Youth Policy Forum.

Ehrle Macomber, Jennifer, Mike Pergamit, Tracy Vericker, Daniel Kuehn, Marla McDaniel, Erica H. Zielewski, Adam Kent, and Heidi Johnson (2009). Multiple Pathways Connecting to School and Work. Washington, DC: Urban Institute.

Esterle, John, and Chris Gates (2010). Civic Pathways Out of Poverty and Into Opportunity. Washington, DC: Philanthropy for Active Civic Engagement.

Fernandez, Adrienne (2007). Vulnerable Youth: Background and Policies. Washington, DC: Congressional Research Service.

Foster-Bey, John, Nathan Dietz, and Robert Grimm, Jr. (2006). Volunteers Mentoring Youth: Implications of Closing the Mentoring Gap. Washington, DC: Corporation for National and Community Service.

Gan, Katherine N., JoAnn Jastrzab, Anna Jefferson, Glen Schneider, and Caroline Shlager (2011). Youth Corps Emerging Practices for Education and Employment. Boston, MA: Abt Associates.

Ganzglass, Evelyn Harris, and Linda Harris (2008). Creating Postsecondary Pathways to Good Jobs for Young High School Dropouts: The Possibilities and the Challenges. Washington, DC: Center for American Progress.

Grimm, Robert, Kevin Cramer, LaMonica Shelton, Nathan Dietz, Lillian Dote, and Shelby Jennings (2008). Still Serving: Measuring the Eight-Year Impact of AmeriCorps on Alumni. Washington, DC: Corporation for National and Community Service.

Grobe, Terry, Kate O'Sullivan, Sally T. Prouty, and Sarah White (2011). A Green Career Pathways Framework: Postsecondary and Employment Success for Low-Income, Disconnected Youth. Washington, DC: The Corps Network.

Grubb, W. Norton (2003). Using Community Colleges to Re-Connect Disconnected Youth. New York: Community College Research Center, Institute on Education and the Economy, Teachers College, Columbia University.

Hair, Elizabeth, Kristin Moore, Thomas Ling, Cameron McPhee-Baker, and Brett Brown (2009). Youth Who are 'Disconnected' and Those Who Then

Reconnect: Assessing the Influence of Family, Programs, Peers and Communities. Washington, DC: Child Trends.

Hanleybrown, Fay, John Kania, and Mark Kramer. "Channeling Change: Making Collective Impact Work." Stanford Social Innovation Review, January 2012 ed.

Hastings, Sara, Rhonda Tsoi-A-Fatt, and Linda Harris (2010). Building a Comprehensive Youth Employment System: Examples of Effective Practice. Washington, DC: Center for Law and Social Policy.

Hooker, S. and Brand, B. (2009). Success at Every Step: How 23 Programs Support Youth on the Path to College and Beyond. Washington, DC: American Youth Policy Forum.

Kania, John, and Mark Kramer. "Collective Impact." Stanford Social Innovation Review, Winter 2011 ed.

KIDS COUNT. Indicator Brief: Reducing the Number of Disconnected Youth (2009). Baltimore, MD: The Annie E. Casey Foundation.

Maguire, Sheila, Joshua Freely, Carol Clymer, Maureen Conway, and Deena Schwartz (2010). Tuning into Local Labor Markets: Findings from the Sectoral Employment Impact Study. Philadelphia, PA: Private/Public Ventures.

Manyika, James, Susan Lund, Byron Auguste, Lenny Mendonca, Tim Welsh, and Sreenivas Ramaswamy (2011). An Economy that Works: Job Creation and America's Future. McKinsey Global Institute.

McKnaught Yonkman, Mary, and John Marshall Bridgeland (2009). All Volunteer Force from Military to Civilian Service. Washington, DC: Civic Enterprises.

Millenky, Megan, Dan Bloom, Sara Muller-Ravett, and Joseph Broadus (2011). Staying on Course: Three-Year Results of the National Guard Youth ChalleNGe Evaluation. New York: MDRC.

O'Connor, Jenn, and Tom Hilliard (2009). Back on Track: Re-Connecting New Yorks Disconnected Youth to Education and Employment. New York: Schuyler Center for Analysis and Advocacy.

O'Connor, Robert (2006). Mentoring in America 2005: A Snapshot of the Current State of Mentoring. Alexandria, VA: MENTOR.

Pathways to Prosperity Project (2011). Pathways to Prosperity: Meeting the Challenge of Preparing Young Americans for the 21st Century. Boston, MA: Harvard Graduate School of Education.

Ready by 21, Credentialed by 26 Series (2011). When Working Works: Employment and Postsecondary Success.

Riley, Michael Chavez (2009). Building a Better Bridge: Helping Youth to Enter and Succeed in College. New York: Youth Development Institute, a Program of the Tides Center.

Saito, Rebecca N., and Dr. Cynthia L. Sipe (2006). The National Agenda for Action: Background and Analysis of Mentoring Today. Alexandria, VA: MENTOR.

Shelton, LaMonica, Brooke Nicholas, Lillian Dote, and Robert Grimm (2007). AmeriCorps: Changing Lives, Changing America – A Report on AmeriCorps' Impact on Members and Non-Profit Organizations. Washington, DC: Corporation for National and Community Service.

Sipe, Cynthia L. (1996). Mentoring: A Synthesis of P/PV's Research 1988-1995. Philadelphia: Private/Public Ventures.

Steinberg, Adria and Cheryl Almeida (2011). Pathway to Recovery: Implementing a Back on Track through College Model. Boston, MA: Jobs for the Future.

Stuhldreher, Anne and Rourke Obrien (2011). Family Independence Initiative: New Approach to Help Families Exit Poverty. Washington, DC: New America Foundation.

Treschan, Lazar, and David Jason Fischer (2009). From Basic Skills to Better Futures: Generating Economic Dividends for New York City. New York: The Community Service Society.

U.S. Census Bureau (2004). Educational Attainment in the United States: 2003 Population Characteristics.

U.S. Congressional Research Service (2009). Disconnected Youth: A Look at 16- to 24- Year Olds Who Are Not Working or In School.

Wald, Michael, and Tia Martinez (2003). Connected by 25: Improving the Life Chances of the Country's Most Vulnerable 14-24 Year Olds. Prepared for William and Flora Hewlett Foundation.

Weeter, C. and Martin, N. (2011). Building Roads to Success: Key Considerations for Communities and States Reconnecting Youth to Education. Washington, DC: National Youth Employment Coalition.

WESTAT and METIS ASSOCIATES (2011). CEO Young Adult Literacy Program and the Impact of Adding Paid Internships: NYC Center for Economic Opportunity Evaluation.

White House Task Force for Disadvantaged Youth (2003). Final Report.

Wight, Vanessa, Michelle Chau, Yumiko Aratani, Susan Wile Schwarz, and Kalyani Thampi (2010). A Profile of Disconnected Young Adults in 2010. New York: National Center for Children of Poverty, Columbia University.

Youth Transition Funders Group (2010). Connected by 25: Effective Policy Solutions for Vulnerable Youth, Issue Brief.

End Notes

[1] The literature, including reports for the U.S. Congress, characterizes young people 16 to 24 years old who are out of school and work as disconnected youth.

[2] Belfield, Clive R., Henry M. Levin, and Rachel Rosen (2012). *The Economic Value of Opportunity Youth.* Washington, DC: Civic Enterprises.

[3] Bridgeland, John M. and Jessica A. Milano (2012). *Opportunity Road: The Promise and Challenges of America's Forgotten Youth.* Washington, DC: Civic Enterprises and America's Promise Alliance.

[4] Bell, David N.F. & Blanchflower, David G., 2011. *Youth Unemployment in Europe and the United States,* IZA Discussion Papers 5673, Institute for the Study of Labor (IZA).; Thomas A. Mroz & Timothy H. Savage, 2006. *The Long-Term Effects of Youth Unemployment,* Journal of Human Resources, University of Wisconsin Press.

[5] Carnevale, A.P., Smith, N. & J. Strohl. 2010. *Help Wanted. Projections of Jobs and Education Requirements through 2018.*

[6] Ibid.

[7] Bridgeland, John M. and Jessica A. Milano (2012). *Opportunity Road: The Promise and Challenges of America's Forgotten Youth.* Washington, DC: Civic Enterprises and America's Promise Alliance.

[8] Bridgeland, John M. and Jessica A. Milano (2012). *Opportunity Road: The Promise and Challenges of America's Forgotten Youth.* Washington, DC: Civic Enterprises and America's Promise Alliance.

[9] *Opportunity Road: The Promise and Challenges of America's Forgotten Youth.*

[10] Corporation for National and Community Service, *Improving Lives and Communities: Perspectives on 40 Years of VISTA Service.* Washington, DC: 2008.

[11] Corporation for National and Community Service, Office of Research and Policy Development, *Still Serving: Measuring the Eight-Year Impact of AmeriCorps on Alumni.* Washington, DC: 2008.

In: Opportunity Youth
Editor: Paris Marina

ISBN: 978-1-63117-415-5
© 2014 Nova Science Publishers, Inc.

Chapter 2

DISCONNECTED YOUTH: A LOOK AT 16- TO 24-YEAR OLDS WHO ARE NOT WORKING OR IN SCHOOL*

Adrienne L. Fernandes-Alcantara and Thomas Gabe

ABSTRACT

Policymakers and youth advocates have begun to focus greater attention on young people who are not working or in school. Generally characterized as "disconnected," these youth may also lack strong social networks that provide assistance in the form of employment connections and other supports such as housing and financial assistance. Without attachment to work or school, disconnected youth may be vulnerable to experiencing negative outcomes as they transition to adulthood. The purpose of the report is to provide context for Congress about the characteristics of disconnected youth, and the circumstances in which they live. These data may be useful as Congress considers policies to retain students in high school and to provide opportunities for youth to obtain job training and employment.

Since the late 1990s, social science research has introduced different definitions of the term "disconnected." Across multiple studies of disconnected youth, the ages of the youth and the length of time they are out of school or work for purposes of being considered disconnected

---

* This is an edited, reformatted and augmented version of the Congressional Research Service Publication, No. R40535, dated December 16, 2011.

differ. In addition, a smaller number of studies have also incorporated incarcerated youth into estimates of the population. Due to these methodological differences, the number of youth who are considered disconnected varies. According to the research, the factors that are associated with disconnection are not entirely clear, though some studies have shown that parental education and receipt of public assistance are influential.

This Congressional Research Service (CRS) analysis expands the existing research on disconnected youth. The analysis uses Current Population Survey (CPS) data to construct a definition of "disconnected." This definition includes noninstitutionalized youth ages 16 through 24 who were not working or in school at the time of the survey (February through April) and did not work or attend school any time during the previous year. The definition is narrower than those used by other studies because it captures youth who are unemployed and not in school for a longer period of time. This is intended to exclude youth who may, in fact, be connected for part or most of a year. Youth who are both married to a connected spouse *and* are parenting are also excluded from the definition. For these reasons, the number and share of youth in the analysis who are considered disconnected are smaller than in some other studies. Still, 2.6 million youth ages 16 through 24—or 6.9% of this population—met the definition of disconnected in 2010, meaning that they were not in school or working for all of 2010 and at some point between February and April of 2011. As expected, rates of disconnection have varied over time depending on economic cycles.

Like the existing research, the CRS analysis finds that a greater share of female and minority youth are disconnected, and that their rates of disconnection have been higher over time. The analysis evaluates some other characteristics that have not been widely studied in the existing research. For instance, compared to their peers in the general population, disconnected youth tend to have fewer years of education, and are more likely to live apart from their parents and to have children. Disconnected youth are also twice as likely to be poor than their connected peers. The analysis further finds that the parents of disconnected youth are more likely than their counterparts to be unemployed and to have lower educational attainment.

Given the state of the current economy, rates of disconnection may remain stable or climb. Policymakers may consider interventions to reconnect youth to work and/or school. Interventions can target children and youth at a particular stage of their early lives. Interventions can also focus on particular institutions or systems, such as the family, community, and schools.

INTRODUCTION

A young person's detachment from both the labor market and school is an indicator that he or she may not be adequately making the transition to adulthood. Referred to as "disconnected" in the social science literature, youth who are not working or in school may have difficulty gaining the skills and knowledge needed to attain self-sufficiency. Without adequate employment, these youth may also lack access to health insurance and disability benefits, and forego the opportunity to build a work history that will contribute to future higher wages and employability. Disconnected youth may also lack strong social networks that provide assistance in the form of employment connections and other supports such as housing and financial assistance.

The purpose of the report is to provide context for Congress about the characteristics of youth who are not working or in school, and the circumstances in which they live. A demographic profile of disconnected youth may be useful for discussions of efforts to improve the outcomes of at-risk high school students, such as through programs authorized by the Elementary and Secondary Education Act (ESEA) of 1965.[1] The topic of disconnected youth may also emerge as Congress explores policies to provide vulnerable youth with job training and employment opportunities, through new or existing programs, including those authorized by the Workforce Investment Act (WIA) of 1998.[2]

Research since the late 1990s has sought to identify and characterize disconnected youth. Based on varying definitions of the term "disconnected" and the methodology used among multiple studies, estimates of the disconnected youth population range. The Congressional Research Service (CRS) conducted an analysis of the U.S. Census Bureau's Annual Social and Economic Supplement (ASEC) to the Current Population Survey (CPS) to more fully understand the characteristics of disconnected youth, and to provide recent data on the population. Based on select questions in the CPS, the analysis constructs a definition of disconnection that includes noninstitutionalized youth ages 16 through 24. This definition includes noninstitutionalized youth ages 16 through 24 who were not working or in school at the time of the survey (February through April 2011) and did not work or attend school any time during the previous year (2010).[3] The CPS surveys individuals in households, and not those in institutional settings, such as college dorms, military quarters, and mental health institutions. (The number and share of disconnected individuals would likely increase significantly if the CRS analysis incorporated data from surveys of prisons and jails.[4] On the other hand, these figures would likely be offset if youth in colleges and the military were counted.)

The CRS definition is narrower than those used by other studies because it captures youth who are unemployed and not in school for a longer period of time. The definition is intended to exclude youth who may, in fact, be connected for part or most of a year, and may be between jobs or taking an extended break after school. Youth who are married to a connected spouse and are parenting are also excluded from the definition, because they are working in the home and can presumably rely on the income of their spouses. For these reasons, the number and share of youth in the analysis who are considered disconnected are smaller than in some other studies. Still, 2.6 million youth ages 16 through 24—or 6.9% of this population—met the definition of disconnected in 2011 (disconnected for all of 2010 and between February and April of 2011).

Like many other studies, the CRS analysis finds that a greater share of female and minority youth tend to be disconnected, although in some recent years rates of disconnection among females and males have been similar or converged. The CRS analysis also evaluates other characteristics that have not been widely studied in the existing research. For instance, compared to their peers in the general population, disconnected youth tend to have fewer years of education and are less likely to have health insurance. They are more likely to live apart from their parents (except for youth ages 22-24) and be poor. Further, the CRS analysis expands upon the existing research by exploring the characteristics of the parents of disconnected and connected youth who reside with their parents. The analysis finds that the parents of disconnected youth are more likely than their counterparts to be unemployed and to have a lower level of educational attainment. Finally, the analysis also examines trends in disconnectedness over time, from 1988 through 2011. It shows that the rates of disconnection have ranged from about 3.9% (in 1999 and 2000) to just over 7.4% (in 2010). Trends in disconnection rates for males and females for the most part run parallel to each other, with disconnection rates for females being consistently higher than those for males over the period except that in 2010, when these rates converged (in the second through fourth months of 2011, women had slightly higher rates). Disconnected rates were also highest over the period for black (non-Hispanic) males in the study. In most years, rates of disconnection were highest among 19-to-21 year olds or 22-to-24 year olds.

The first section of this report discusses Congress' growing interest in issues around youth who are not working or in school. The second section presents a brief overview of research on the population, including the number of disconnected youth, characteristics of the population, as well as the factors that have been associated with disconnection. The purpose of this section is to show the variation in the research on the population and to suggest that the definition of "disconnected" is fluid. (The report does not evaluate the methodology or validity of these studies, or discuss in great detail the federal programs or policies that may be available to assist disconnected youth.)[5] The third section presents the CRS analysis of disconnected youth ages 16 through 24. The final section discusses implications for future research and federal policy. **Appendix A** provides a summary of the major studies on disconnected youth. **Appendix B** and **Appendix C** present the data tables that accompany this analysis.

BACKGROUND

Congress has taken interest in, and enacted, policies that can assist youth who are not working or in school. The 110th Congress conducted a hearing on disconnected youth and considered legislation that was intended to assist this population. The hearing was conducted by the House Ways and Means Subcommittee on Income Security and Family Support.[6] The purpose of the hearing was to explore the pathways that lead young people to become detached from work, school, housing, and important social networks; and to learn about the existing and potential programs targeted to this population. Social science researchers and other witnesses asserted that youth are most vulnerable to becoming disconnected during downturns in the economy, and that educational attainment and skills can mitigate the challenges they might face in securing employment in an increasingly competitive global market.[7] They further stated that the federal government has a vested interest in connecting youth to school and work because of the potential costs incurred in their adulthood in the form of higher transfer payments and social support expenses, as well as lost tax revenue.[8]

Also in the 110th Congress, the House Education and Labor Committee examined how the federal government can help to re-engage disconnected youth. At the request of the committee, the Government Accountability Office (GAO) issued a report in February 2008 that reviewed the characteristics and elements that make local programs funded with federal dollars successful in re-engaging youth, as well as the challenges in operating such programs.[9] The report defined disconnected youth as those youth ages 14 to 24 who are not working or in school, or who lack family or other support networks.[10] It found that programs were successful because of effective staff and leadership; a holistic approach to serving youth that addresses the youth's multiple and individual needs; design of the programs, such as experiential learning opportunities and self-paced curricula; and a focus on developing youth's leadership skills. The report further found that local programs reported challenges such as the complex life circumstances of the youth, including learning disabilities, violence in their communities, and lack of adequate transportation; gaps in services, such as housing and mental health services; funding constraints; and managing federal grants with different reporting requirements.

The 110th Congress also marked the first time that multiple bills were introduced to target youth identified as "disconnected." The legislation generally referred to disconnected youth as individuals ages 16 to 26 (or ages in between) who were not in school nor working; and/or who were part of a population of vulnerable youth, such as youth in foster care, runaway and homeless youth,[11] incarcerated youth, and minority youth from poor communities.[12] The bills' proposed interventions involved changes to existing workforce or educational programs, creation of new programs, or modifications in the tax code to encourage employers to hire youth who are not working or in school. One of the bills—the College Opportunity and Affordability Act of 2008 (H.R. 4137)—was signed into law (P.L. 110-315). P.L. 110-315 did not include a definition of disconnected youth, but identified "disconnected students" as those who are—limited English proficient, from groups that are traditionally underrepresented in postsecondary education, students with disabilities, students who are homeless children and youths, and students who are in or aging out of foster care. The law made these students and "other disconnected students" (not defined) eligible for programs authorized by the Higher Education Act, including the TRIO programs, which provide college preparation and other services for low-income high school students who are the first in their families to attend college.[13]

The American Recovery and Reinvestment Act of 2009 (P.L. 111-5), the omnibus law that provided federal funding for programs to encourage economic recovery, included provisions that pertain to disconnected youth.[14] Of the $1.2 billion appropriated for programs in the Workforce Investment Act, Congress extended the age through which youth are eligible for year-round activities (from age 21 to age 24) so that job training programs would be available for "young adults who have become disconnected from both education and the labor market." In addition, the law made businesses who employ youth defined as "disconnected" eligible for the Work Opportunity

Tax Credit (WOTC). According to the law, a disconnected youth, for purposes of WOTC, is an individual certified as being between the ages 16 and 25 on the hiring date; not regularly attending any secondary, technical, or post-secondary school during the six-month period preceding the hiring date; not regularly employed during the six-month period preceding the hiring date; and not readily employable by reason of lacking a sufficient number of skills. Youth with low levels of formal education "may satisfy the requirement that an individual is not readily employable by reason of lacking a sufficient number of skills."

Given the slow job growth following the 2007-2009 recession, Congress may continue to pursue job creation and retention strategies, including for youth who face dim prospects in securing employment.[15] The next section provides an overview of the existing research of disconnected youth, and it is followed by the CRS analysis. Research on disconnected youth can provide context for Congress regarding the magnitude of the population and the challenges they face.

OVERVIEW OF RESEARCH ON DISCONNECTED YOUTH

CRS reviewed nine studies on disconnected youth from 1999 through 2007. These studies were identified by searching social science periodicals, consulting the GAO team involved in the disconnected youth study, and reviewing works' cited pages in a few of the studies. The nine studies were carried out by federal agencies or non-governmental organizations. Below is a brief overview of the studies' methodologies, definitions of the population, as well as findings. Appendix A summarizes the studies. This review does not evaluate the methodology or validity of studies on disconnected youth.

Methodology and Number of Disconnected Youth

Across the nine studies, figures of disconnected youth vary because of their methodology, the age range of youth, and the period of time examined.[16] Most of the studies were cross-sectional, meaning that they considered youth to be disconnected at a particular point in time—usually on a given day survey data were collected—or over a period of time, such as anytime during a previous year or the entire previous year. Some, however, were longitudinal, and tracked a youth's connection to work and school over multiple years. The studies also used varying data sets, including the Current Population Survey, Decennial Census, National Longitudinal Survey of Youth (NLSY, which includes a 1979 cohort and a 1997 cohort), and the American Community Survey (ACS). Most of the studies did not provide actual numbers of disconnected youth, and instead reported percentages. Percentages ranged from 7% to 20% of the youth population, depending on the ages of the youth and methodology. Among the few studies that provided estimates of the actual number, they found that about 1.4 million to five million youth were disconnected. One oft-cited study found that on average, 5.2 million youth ages 16 to 24, or 16.4% of that age group, were not working or in school at a given point in time.[17]

The studies counted youth as young as age 16 and as old as age 24, with ages in between (e.g., 16 to 19, 18 to 24).[18] Youth were considered disconnected for most of the studies if they met the definition at a particular point in time, though for one study, youth were considered disconnected if they met the criteria in the first month they were surveyed and in at least eight of the eleven following months.[19] Another used a definition of disconnected to include youth who were not working or in school for at least the previous year before the youth were surveyed, in 1999.[20] Some of the studies' definitions incorporated other characteristics, such as marital status and educational attainment. For example, an analysis of NLSY97 data used a definition of disconnected youth that counts only those youth who were not in school or working, and not married.[21] Two other studies used a definition for 18- to 24-year olds who were not enrolled in school, not working, and who had obtained, at most, a high school diploma.[22] Further, nearly all of the studies used definitions that included only non-institutionalized youth. This means that the studies did not count youth in prisons, juvenile justice facilities, mental health facilities, college dorms, military facilities, and other institutions. However, two studies incorporated incarcerated youth and/or youth in the armed forces.[23] Inclusion of youth living in institutional settings could affect the number and share of youth considered as disconnected. Adding youth who are in prison or juvenile justice facilities would increase the number of disconnected youth, whereas adding youth who are living in school dorms or in the armed forces would increase the number of connected youth.

As mentioned in the section above, the College Cost Reduction Act (P.L. 110-315) did not define "disconnected youth" but identified certain vulnerable youth—such as runaway and homeless youth and English language learners—as being "disconnected students," and therefore eligible for certain educational support services. One of the studies classified disconnected youth in the same vein. The study defined groups of disadvantaged youth ages 14 to 17, including those involved with the juvenile justice system and youth in foster care, as vulnerable to becoming disconnected (or having long-term spells of unemployment) because of the negative outcomes these groups tend to face as a whole.[24]

Other Characteristics

In all studies that examined gender, an equal or greater share of females were disconnected. According to one analysis of CPS data, disconnected youth included individuals age 16 through 19, and not in school or working (at what appears to be a particular point in time).[25] The study found that during select years from 1986 through 2006, approximately 7% to 10% of youth met this definition annually. Females were slightly more likely to be disconnected than males in 2006—8.1% compared to 7.1%. Another analysis of CPS data calculated the number and share of disconnected youth based on data collected from monthly CPS surveys for 2001.[26] The study found that 18% of females and 11% of males were disconnected. About 44% of youth defined as disconnected had dropped out of high school.

Of the studies that examined race and ethnicity, white and Asian youth were less likely to be disconnected than their counterparts of other racial and ethnic groups. According to an analysis of 2009 ACS data, the rates of disconnection among youth ages 16 to 19 by racial category were as follows: 5% of non-Hispanic Asian and Pacific Islanders; 7% of non-Hispanic whites; 12% of Hispanics; and 13% of non-Hispanic blacks.[27]

Reasons Associated with Disconnection

The factors that contribute to disconnection are not entirely clear, though some research has shown that parental education and receipt of public assistance, as well as race and ethnicity, play a role. An analysis of NLSY97 data found that disconnection was associated with being black and parental receipt of government aid from the time the parent was 18 (or their first child was born).[28] A separate analysis of NLSY79 data found that long-term disconnected youth—who were not working or in school for at least 26 weeks in three or more years, and not married—tended to have certain personal and family background factors, including family poverty, family welfare receipt, and low parent education.[29] For example, among young men who met the long-term definition of disconnected, 35% were from poor families, compared to 10% of connected men; 26% were from families receiving welfare (versus 6% of connected men); 28% were from single-parent families (versus 13%); and 45% had a parent who lacked a high school degree (versus 16%). (Corresponding data for females are not available.) The study also found that nearly 90% of those who were disconnected at age 20 to 23 were first disconnected as teenagers. Finally, another study found that teens from low-income families were more likely to be neither enrolled in school nor employed than those from higher-income families, and that teens whose parents did not finish high school were twice as likely to be disengaged than those whose parents have at least some education (actual figures were not provided).[30]

The next section discusses the CRS analysis of disconnected youth.

CRS ANALYSIS OF DISCONNECTED YOUTH

Overview

The CRS analysis expands upon the existing research of disconnected youth. As discussed further below, the CRS definition of disconnected youth is more narrow than most definitions employed by other studies because it captures those who are not working and not in school for a longer period of time (versus at a point in time, or for instance, over a six-month period). This definition is intended to exclude youth who may, in fact, be connected for part or most of a year, and may be between jobs or taking an extended break after school. Unlike all of the other studies, youth who are married to a connected spouse *and* are parenting are also excluded from the definition, based on the assumption that these young people work in the home by caring for their children and rely on financial and social support from their spouses.[31] For these reasons, the number and share of youth in the analysis who are considered disconnected are smaller than in some other studies. Still, as discussed below, 2.6 million youth ages 16 through 24—or 6.9% of this population— meet the definition of disconnected. Further, in contrast to most other studies, the CRS analysis examines the characteristics of the parents of disconnected youth. The analysis finds that they are more likely than the parents of connected youth to be unemployed and have a lower level of educational attainment. The CRS analysis constructs a definition of disconnected youth based on questions asked in the U.S. Census Bureau's Current Population Survey about workforce participation, school attendance, marital, and parental status. The definition includes young people ages 16 through 24 who did not work anytime during a previous year (2010) due primarily to a reason other than school and who also were not working nor in school at the time of the survey (February through April of 2011). (Reasons given as to why youth were not working could include that they were either out of the workforce because they were ill or disabled, taking care of home or family, could not find work, or some other unspecified reason.) This means that youth would be disconnected for a minimum of 12 months (all of 2010), and some or all of a possible additional three months (February through April of 2011). The analysis includes youth as young as 16 because at this age they may begin working and starting to prepare for post-secondary education. The study also includes older youth, up to age 24, since they are in the process of transitioning to adulthood. Many young people in their mid-20s attend school or begin to work, and some live with their parents or other relatives. According to social science research, multiple factors—including delayed age of first marriage, the high cost of living independently, and additional educational opportunities—have extended the period of transition from adolescence to adulthood.[32]

Limitations

One limitation of this analysis is that the CPS surveys individuals in households, and not those in institutional settings, such as prisons, jails, college dorms, military quarters, and mental health institutions. Based on incarceration data from other studies (see **Appendix A**), the number and share of disconnected individuals would likely increase significantly if the study incorporated data from surveys of prisons and jails. Further, the CPS does not count persons who are homeless. While the precise number of homeless youth ages 16 through 24 is unknown, a significant share of these youth may meet the definition of disconnected.[33] On the other hand, the share of disconnected youth in the population might be offset by including members of the armed forces and college students in dorms who are ages 18 through 24, and are by definition, working or going to school. Another limitation of the analysis is that it does not account for the strong possibility that while some disconnected youth are not formally employed, they are likely finding ways to make ends meet through informal markets and social networks. These networks can provide cash assistance, temporary housing and employment, and child care, among other supports. Nonetheless, informal networks are likely unstable, and may not necessarily lead to longer-term employment or attachment to school.[34] As discussed in the section below, nearly half of all disconnected youth live in poverty. Finally, the CRS definition of disconnected youth does not identify those youth who are disconnected for periods that exceed 16 months. As one of the longitudinal studies in **Appendix A** shows, youth are disconnected for three years or more are more likely to face negative outcomes than their counterparts who are disconnected for part of one to two years.[35]

Findings

This section begins with an overview of the reasons disconnected youth said they were not working or in school at any time in 2010. Following this discussion is an overview of the basic demographics of disconnected youth and their characteristics across several domains— educational attainment, living arrangements, parenting status, health insurance coverage, and poverty status. These data, drawn from the 2010 CPS, are compared to data for connected youth. The section ends with a presentation of trend data on disconnection from 1988 through 2010, with a focus on gender, age, and race and ethnicity. Appendix B presents detailed tables of the 2011 data alone and Appendix C provides detailed tables of the trend data.

Reasons Reported for Youth Not Being in School or Working

Figure 1 displays the reasons given for out-of-school youth not working in the first quarter of 2011. Major reasons include taking care of family or home, illness or disability, or that they could not find work. Just under 30% (about 733,000) of disconnected youth were reported to be taking care of home or family and were not disabled. Of those, over half (372,000) were reported as having a child. The CPS does not prompt respondents to elaborate on the type of care provided in the home or to family, and therefore, it is unclear the extent to which this care would interfere with their ability to work or attend school. Illness or disability was reported as the major reason why about 30% (about 799,000) of disconnected youth did not work in 2011, with most designated as having a severe disability.[36] One indication that a person is severely disabled is their receipt of Supplemental Security Income (SSI) or Medicare.[37] Over two-fifths of disconnected individuals with disabilities (345,00) received one of these two benefits, accounting for about one in seven (14.5%) of all disconnected youth. Finally, 42% (1.1 million) could not find work and they did not have a disability or responsibilities in the home; most of these individuals *did not* have a child (1.0 million).

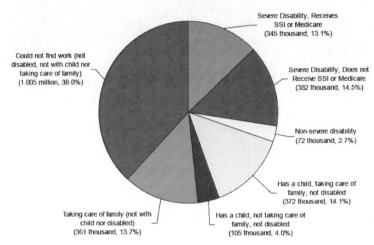

Source: Congressional Research Service based on analysis of data from the U.S. Census Bureau 2011 Current Population Survey (CPS) Annual Social and Economic Supplement (ASEC).

Notes: Disconnected youth are youth who were not working or in school at the time of the survey and were reported as having not worked during the previous year for reasons other than going to school.

Figure 1. Disconnected Youth Ages 16-24, by Disability Status, Presence of Children, and Family Caretaking Responsibility, 2011.

Characteristics of Disconnected Youth

Table 1 compares demographic characteristics of disconnected and connected peers ages 16 through 24 in 2011 (which meant that youth were disconnected in all of 2010 and at the time of the survey in 2011). The table shows that 2.6 million of these youth, or 6.9% of the population, met the definition of disconnected. Further, females and minority youth were more likely than their counterparts to be disconnected. The rate of disconnection among black (non-Hispanic) youth was highest—at 10.4%. Among youth ages 16 through 18, 19 through 21, and 22 through 24, the younger youth were more likely than their older peers to be connected. Finally, relative to connected youth, disconnected youth were more likely to have lower education attainment, to live apart from their parents, be poor, and lack health insurance. These findings are discussed in greater detail below.

Table 1. Summary Characteristics of Connected and Disconnected Youth Ages 16-24, 2011 (Numbers in 1,000s)

	Total number	Disconnected			Connected	
		Number	Percent	Share of total youth	Number	Percent
Age and Gender Age						
Total	38,374	2,641	100.0%	6.9%	35,733	100.0%
Age 16 - 18	13,096	434	16.4%	3.3%	12,662	35.4%
Age 19 - 21	12,607	1,053	39.9%	8.3%	11,555	32.3%
Age 22 - 24	12,671	1,155	43.7%	9.1%	11,517	32.2%
Males						
Total	19,585	1,254	100.0%	6.4%	18,330	100.0%
Age 16 - 18	6,725	209	16.6%	3.1%	6,516	35.5%
Age 19 - 21	6,389	523	41.7%	8.2%	5,866	32.0%
Age 22 - 24	6,471	523	41.7%	8.1%	5,949	32.5%
Females						
Total	18,790	1,387	100.0%	7.4%	17,402	100.0%
Age 16 - 18	6,371	226	16.3%	3.5%	6,146	35.3%
Age 19 - 21	6,219	530	38.2%	8.5%	5,689	32.7%
Age 22 - 24	6,200	632	45.6%	10.2%	5,568	32.0%
Race and Ethnicity by Gender						
Males and Females						
Total	38,374	2,641	100.0%	6.9%	35,733	100.0%
White non-Hispanic	22,638	1,279	48.4%	5.6%	21,359	59.8%
Black non-Hispanic	5,438	567	21.5%	10.4%	4,870	13.6%
Hispanic	7,573	621	23.5%	8.2%	6,953	19.5%
Other, non-Hispanic	2,726	174	6.6%	6.4%	2,551	7.1%
Males						
Total	19,585	1,254	100.0%	6.4%	18,330	100.0%
White non-Hispanic	11,480	617	49.2%	5.4%	10,863	59.3%
Black non-Hispanic	2,645	274	21.8%	10.3%	2,371	12.9%
Hispanic	4,086	286	22.8%	7.0%	3,801	20.7%
Other, non-Hispanic	1,374	78	6.2%	5.7%	1,296	7.1%
Females						
Total	18,790	1,387	100.0%	7.4%	17,402	100.0%
White non-Hispanic	11,157	662	47.7%	5.9%	10,496	60.3%
Black non-Hispanic	2,793	294	21.2%	10.5%	2,499	14.4%
Hispanic	3,487	335	24.2%	9.6%	3,152	18.1%
Other, non-Hispanic	1,352	96	7.0%	7.1%	1,255	7.2%
Education Among Youth Over Age 18						
All Levels of Education						
Total	25,279	2,207	100.0%	8.7%	23,071	100.0%
Age 19 - 21	12,607	1,053	100.0%	8.3%	11,555	100.0%
Age 22 - 24	12,671	1,155	100.0%	9.1%	11,517	100.0%
Lacks High School Diploma or GED						
Total	3,001	669	30.3%	22.3%	2,332	10.1%

	Total number	Disconnected			Connected	
		Number	Percent	Share of total youth	Number	Percent
Age 19 – 21	1,758	332	31.6%	18.9%	1,425	12.3%
Age 22 - 24	1,244	337	29.2%	27.1%	907	7.9%
High School Diploma or GED						
Only						
Total	7,615	1,102	49.9%	14.5%	6,513	28.2%
Age 19 - 21	4,089	584	55.4%	14.3%	3,505	30.3%
Age 22 - 24	3,527	519	44.9%	14.7%	3,008	26.1%
High School Diploma or GED and Additional Schooling						
Total	14,662	436	19.8%	3.0%	14,226	61.7%
Age 19 - 21	6,761	137	13.0%	2.0%	6,624	57.3%
Age 22 - 24	7,901	299	25.9%	3.8%	7,601	66.0%
Living Arrangements by Age						
All Arrangements						
Total	38,374	2,641	100.0%	6.9%	35,733	100.0%
16 - 18	13,096	434	100.0%	3.3%	12,662	100.0%
19 - 21	12,607	1,053	100.0%	8.3%	11,555	100.0%
22 - 24	12,671	1,155	100.0%	9.1%	11,517	100.0%
Lives with one or both parents						
Total	26,203	1,543	58.4%	5.9%	24,659	69.0%
16 - 18	12,093	351	80.9%	2.9%	11,742	92.7%
19 - 21	8,674	626	59.5%	7.2%	8,048	69.7%
22 - 24	5,435	565	49.0%	10.4%	4,870	42.3%
Lives apart from parents						
Total	12,172	1,098	41.6%	9.0%	11,073	31.0%
16 - 18	1,002	83	19.1%	8.3%	920	7.3%
19 - 21	3,933	426	40.5%	10.8%	3,507	30.3%
22 - 24	7,236	589	51.0%	8.1%	6,647	57.7%
Poverty Status						
Total	38,374	2,641	100.0%	6.9%	35,733	100.0%
Poor	8,111	1,285	48.6%	15.8%	6,826	19.1%
Nonpoor	30,263	1,356	51.4%	4.5%	28,907	80.9%
Health Insurance Coverage Status						
Total	38,374	2,641	100.0%	6.9%	35,733	100.0%
Without health insurance coverage	9,182	1,012	38.3%	11.0%	8,170	22.9%
With health insurance coverage	29,192	1,629	61.7%	5.6%	27,563	77.1%

Source: Congressional Research Service based on analysis of data from the U.S. Census Bureau 2011 Current Population Survey (CPS) Annual Social and Economic Supplement (ASEC).

Notes: Disconnected youth are youth who were not working or in school at the time of the survey and were reported as having not worked during the previous year for reasons other than going to school.

Gender and Age

It might be expected that a higher percentage of males than females are disconnected, given that a greater share of males ages 16 through 24 have dropped out of high school[38] and that males appear to be more vulnerable to losing jobs.[39] However, consistent with other studies of disconnected youth, the CRS analysis shows that females are more likely than males to be disconnected. Still, the difference in the rates between males and females ages 16 through 24 is relatively small—7.4% of females and 6.4% of males, as depicted in **Figure 2**.

The higher rates for females appears to be explained by the fact they were more likely to be parenting.[40] Overall, 2.8% of females and 0.3% of males were parenting. It is possible that their parenting responsibilities kept them from working or attending school. (As shown in **Figure 1**, about 14% of youth reported they were not connected in 2011 because they were taking care of home or family, and had children.) If the share of females with children is removed from each of the age categories, females ages 16 through 18 are just as likely as those ages 19 through 21 to be disconnected, and females ages 22 through 24 are *less likely* to be disconnected as their male counterparts without children (which is nearly all the males).

Further, rates of disconnection increase with age for both females and males. Approximately 3% to 4% of males and females ages 16 through 18 were disconnected, presumably because younger youth are more likely to be attending high school. These rates were more than twice as high among older youth ages 19 through 21, and 22 through 24.

Race and Ethnicity

Minority youth are more likely than their white peers to not be working or in school.[41] **Figure 3** shows rates of disconnection by race and ethnicity, gender, and parental status for 2011. Non-Hispanic black females had the highest rates of disconnection (10.5%), compared to 9.6% of Hispanic females and 5.9% of white females. The same was true among males: 10.3% of blacks, 7.0% of Hispanics, and 5.4% of non-Hispanic whites were disconnected.

Parenting status appears to account for the difference in disconnection between non-Hispanic white males and females and between non-Hispanic black males and females. If the share of white and black females with children is removed from the calculation, females would be *less* likely to be disconnected than their male counterparts without children (which is nearly all the males).

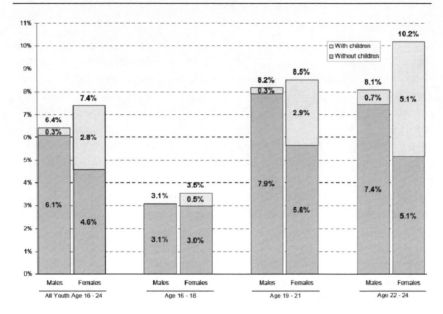

Figure 2. Disconnected Rates Among Youth Ages 16-24, by Age Group, Gender, and Parental Status, 2011.

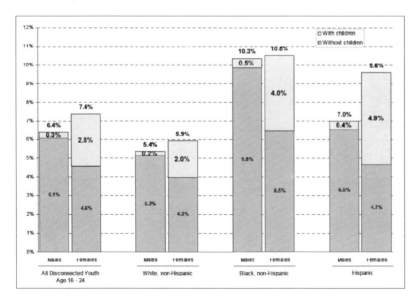

Figure 3. Disconnected Rates Among Youth Ages 16-24, by Race, Ethnicity, Gender, and Parental Status, 2011.

Educational Attainment

CRS evaluated the educational attainment of disconnected youth who were old enough to have completed high school relative to their connected peers, based on questions in the CPS about highest level of education completed. Youth ages 19 through 24 were grouped according to whether they (1) lacked a high school diploma or general education development (GED) certificate; (2) had a high school diploma or GED; or (3) graduated from high school and had additional schooling beyond high school. Higher educational attainment is associated with higher earnings, and earnings differences have grown over time among workers with different levels of educational attainment. In 2010, higher earnings and lower unemployment rates were associated with higher educational attainment among persons 25 and older.[42] For example, the median weekly earnings for those with less than a high school diploma was $444 and their unemployment rate was 14.9%. The corresponding figures for high school graduates was $626 and 10.3%, respectively. Among those with a bachelor's degree, the corresponding figures were $1,038 and 5.4%, respectively. [43]

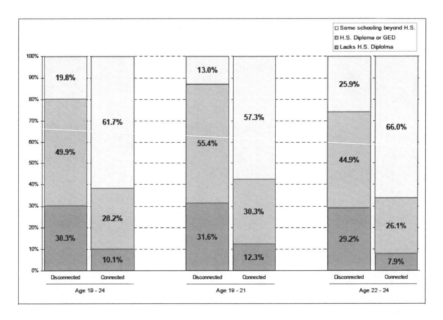

Figure 4. Educational Attainment of Connected and Disconnected Youth Ages 19-24, by Age Group, 2011.

As a group, disconnected youth appear to be at a disadvantage in competing for jobs that pay higher wages because of their comparatively low levels of education. **Figure 4** displays the share of disconnected and connected youth by age (19-24, 19-21, and 22-24) within the three categories of educational attainment. Disconnected youth tend to have fewer years of schooling than their connected counterparts. In 2011, among 19 through 21-year olds, nearly one-third (31.6%) disconnected youth lacked a diploma or GED, compared to about one out of ten (12.3%) connected youth. Among older youth, this difference persisted, with 29.2% of disconnected youth and 7.9% of connected youth lacking a diploma or GED.

Poverty

Poverty may be both a cause and consequence of youth disconnectedness. Growing up poor may contribute to the likelihood that a child will be disconnected in making the transition from adolescence to adulthood. In turn, being disconnected may contribute to youth being poor, especially among youth who are no longer living at home with parents or other family members to contribute to their support.

The analysis of poverty in this section is based on 2010 income of related family members in a household as reported as part of the CPS for 2011. Income includes pre-tax money income from all sources, including wages, salaries, and benefits, such as unemployment compensation and Supplemental Security Income (SSI). Youth were considered poor if their annual family pre-tax money income in 2010 fell below Census Bureau poverty income thresholds. Poverty thresholds vary by family size and composition. A youth living alone, with no other family members, would be considered poor in the previous year if his/her pre-tax money income was under $11,344; for a youth under age 18 living with a single parent and no other related family members, the youth and his/her parent would be considered poor if their family income was below $15,030; and, for a youth over age 18 living with both parents and a younger sibling (under age 18), and no other related family members, they would be considered poor if their family income was below $22,113.[44] **Figure 5** shows that in 2010, 45.7% of all disconnected youth were poor, compared to 17.8% of their connected peers. While rates of poverty for connected youth were stable across age groups, poverty increased with age for disconnected youth. Just over half of youth age 22 through 24 were poor, compared to 33.8% of youth ages 16 through 18 and 44.5% of youth ages 19 through 21. The rates of poverty among connected youth were stable at 17.0% to 18.5% across the three age groups.

Poverty status appears to be strongly correlated with educational attainment. This is not surprising, given that higher rates of educational attainment are associated with greater job attachment and higher wages. Of course, by the definition of disconnected youth used in this analysis, none were working in 2010, so none had earnings. Connected youth were working or in school, and presumably drawing income from their jobs, or financial aid. Parental or other income may also contribute to their support, even when youth are no longer living at home. **Figure 6** shows the percentage of poor disconnected and connected youth ages 19 through 24 by educational attainment. Disconnected youth in each grouping of educational attainment—lacks high school diploma, high school diploma or GED, or some schooling beyond high school—were two to three times more likely to be poor than connected youth.

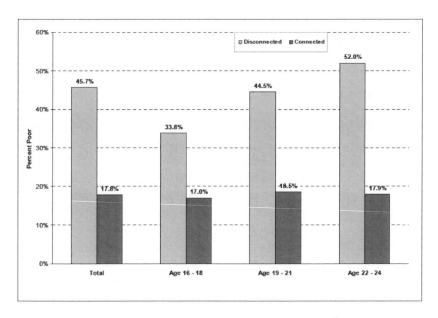

Figure 5. Poverty Status of Disconnected and Connected Youth Ages 16-24, by Age Group 2011. (Poverty Status Based on Family Income in 2010).

Still, higher educational attainment appears to have provided disconnected youth with more of a buffer from poverty. The rate of poverty was higher among disconnected youth without a high school diploma (60.4%) than among their disconnected counterparts with more education (36.3% to 49.5%). Yet even disconnected youth with some schooling beyond high school were more likely than connected youth lacking a high school diploma to be poor, 49.5% and 37.4% respectively.

Poverty by family living arrangement is presented later in this report and implications of poverty and disconnected youth are discussed further in the conclusion.

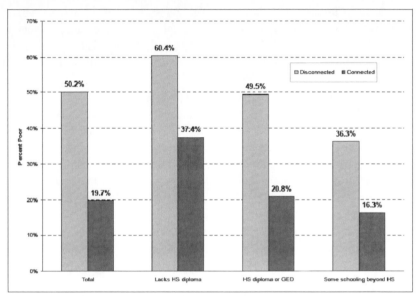

Source: Congressional Research Service based on analysis of data from the U.S. Census Bureau 2011 Current Population Survey (CPS) Annual Social and Economic Supplement (ASEC). See Table B-6 in Appendix B for greater detail.

Notes: Disconnected youth are youth who were not working or in school at the time of the survey and were reported as having not worked during the previous year for reasons other than going to school.

Figure 6. Poverty Status of Disconnected and Connected Youth Ages 19-24, by Level of Educational Attainment, 2011. (Poverty Status Based on Family Income in 2010).

Health Insurance

Health insurance is considered important because of the well-documented, far-reaching consequences of being uninsured.[45] For instance, uninsured persons are more likely to forgo needed health care than people with health coverage and are less likely to have a "usual source of care," that is, a person or place identified as the source to which the patient usually goes for health services or medical advice (not including emergency rooms). Having a usual source is important because people who establish ongoing relationships with health care providers or facilities are more likely to access preventive health services and have regular visits with a physician, compared with individuals without a usual source.

The CRS analysis examined the share of disconnected and connected youth without health insurance by age. In the CPS, respondents report whether they have private insurance (i.e., employer-sponsored, direct-purchase, or self employment-based plans) or public insurance (i.e. Medicaid, Medicare, Children's Health Insurance Program (CHIP), and military health care, among other types of coverage). **Figure 7** shows the share of disconnected and connected youth without health insurance, based on being without health insurance coverage for all of 2010.

Overall, rates of uninsurance were relatively high for both disconnected youth (38.3%) and connected youth (22.9%). Yet disconnected youth were about one third more likely than connected youth to be uninsured. This is not surprising given that they are not eligible for employer-sponsored health insurance. Most Americans obtain health coverage through the workplace. In 2010, approximately 195.9 million persons had employment-based health insurance, which accounts for 55.3% of the total population.[46] It might be expected that an even greater share of disconnected youth would lack coverage; however, some youth are likely covered by their parents' health insurance plans, or through CHIP or another government health insurance program for low-income individuals (CRS did not examine coverage type among youth). As shown in **Figure 1**, above, about 345,000 (13.1%) of disconnected youth receive SSI or Medicare because of a disability. A majority of states provide Medicaid coverage for those individuals eligible for SSI.[47]

Uninsured rates increase for both connected and disconnected youth as they age. Nearly 20% (18.9%) of disconnected youth ages 16 through 18, 38.9% of disconnected youth ages 19 through 21, and 45.0% of disconnected youth ages 22 through 24 were uninsured. This is compared to 13.2%, 25.7%, and 30.6% of connected youth the same age, respectively. The youngest youth may have had lower uninsured rates because they were covered under their parents' plan or qualify for CHIP or Medicaid. However, as health plans implement the requirement to cover children up to age 26—even those children who are married—the difference in coverage rates may narrow between these age groups. [48]

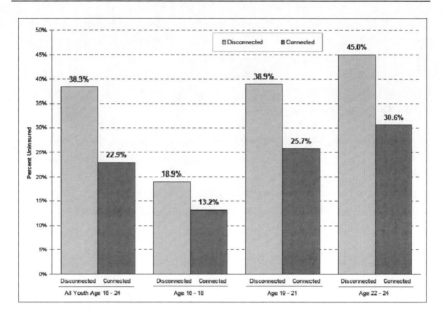

Figure 7. Disconnected and Connected Youth Ages 16-24 Without Health Insurance Coverage by Age Group, 2011. (Health Insurance Status During All of 2010).

Living Arrangements

A growing body of social science research suggests that the transition to adulthood for young people today is becoming longer and more complex.[49] During this period, youth rely heavily on their families for financial support, and many continue to live with their parents beyond the traditional age of high school. Disconnected youth, however, may be less likely than their peers to rely on supports from their parents. A 2008 study by the Government Accountability Office would suggest this. GAO included in its definition of the disconnected population those youth "who lack family or other social supports."[50]

The CRS analysis evaluated whether disconnected youth were more or less likely to live with one or both parents. This analysis is based on responses to CPS questions about living alone or with parent(s), another family member, spouse, and/or non-relative. As shown in **Figure 8**, overall, about four out of ten disconnected youth and three out of ten connected youth did not live with one or both parents in 2011. (This translates to about 1.1 million disconnected youth and 11.1 million connected youth.) While disconnected youth as a whole were less likely to live with one or both parents (58.5%, compared to

69.1% of connected youth), a larger share of the oldest disconnected youth—those ages 22 through 24—lived at home. Given that many disconnected youth are not earning income and may not have strong social networks, they may have no other choice but to live at home. Reciprocally, it appears that their connected older peers are "fledging," and beginning to become financially independent from their families.

The family structure of disconnected youth who live at home tends to differ from that of their peers. Connected youth who lived at home were more likely to live with both parents (46.6%) than disconnected youth (29.4%).[51] The social science research indicates that children who grow up in mother-only families (or with their mother and step-father) are more likely than children raised with both biological parents to have certain negative outcomes, including poverty-level incomes.[52]

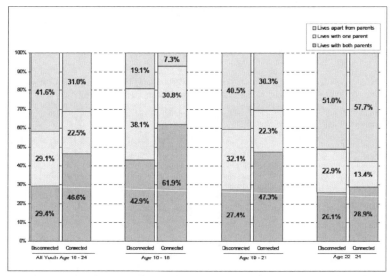

Source: Congressional Research Service based on analysis of data from the U.S. Census Bureau 2011 Current Population Survey (CPS) Annual Social and Economic Supplement (ASEC). See Table B-8 and Table B-9 in Appendix B for greater detail.

Notes: Disconnected youth are youth who were not working or in school at the time of the survey and were reported as having not worked during the previous year for reasons other than going to school.

Figure 8. Living Arrangements of Disconnected and Connected Youth Ages 16-24, by Age Group, 2011.

Figure 9 depicts youth poverty status by living arrangement. The figure shows that disconnected youth are more likely to be poor than are their connected counterparts, even when controlling for living arrangement. Among youth living with both parents, disconnected youth were almost three times more likely than connected youth to be poor (17.4% versus 6.2%, respectively). Poverty rates were higher for youth living in single-parent families than in dual-parent families, but the poverty rate of disconnected youth in single-parent families (47.4%) was almost twice that of connected youth living in such families (24.5%). Poverty rates were highest among youth living apart from their parents; among disconnected youth about seven in ten were poor (71.6%), a rate, again, about twice as high as connected youth (34.6%).

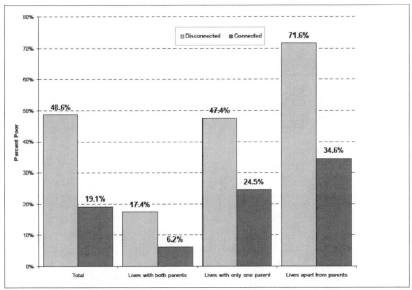

Source: Congressional Research Service based on analysis of data from the U.S. Census Bureau 2011 Current Population Survey (CPS) Annual Social and Economic Supplement (ASEC). See Table B-10 in Appendix B for greater detail.

Notes: Disconnected youth are youth who were not working or in school at the time of the survey and were reported as having not worked during the previous year for reasons other than going to school.

Figure 9. Poverty Status of Disconnected and Connected Youth Ages 16 to 24, by Living Arrangement, 2011. (Poverty Status Based on Family Income in 2010).

Characteristics of Parents Living with Disconnected Youth

The CPS asks only about those individuals who reside in the same household. Therefore, the CRS analysis was able to evaluate only the characteristics of the parents of connected and disconnected youth if they resided together. Approximately 1.5 million disconnected youth, or 58.4% of the disconnected population, lived with their parents (compared to 69.0% of connected youth).

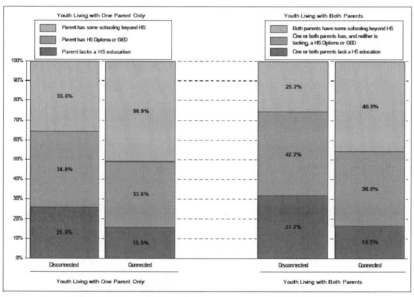

Source: Congressional Research Service based on analysis of data from the U.S. Census Bureau 2011 Current Population Survey (CPS) Annual Social and Economic Supplement (ASEC). See Table B-11 in Appendix B for greater detail.

Notes: Disconnected youth are youth who were not working or in school at the time of the survey and were reported as having not worked during the previous year for reasons other than going to school.

Figure 10. Educational Attainment of Disconnected and Connected Youths' Parents, for Youth Ages 16-24 Living with One or Both Parents, 2011.

The CRS analysis evaluated the education and employment status of parents at a point in time in 2011. The analysis examined this status among parents of youth in single-parent and dual-parent households. **Figure 10** presents information about the educational attainment of parents of disconnected and connected youth. Parents were categorized based on whether they (1) lacked a high school diploma or its equivalent; (2) had a high school diploma or its equivalent; or (3) graduated high school and had additional schooling. Among both youth living with one parent only *and* youth living with both parents, the parents of disconnected youth were much more likely than parents of connected youth to lack a high school diploma or its equivalent.

Further, among single-parent households, 35.6% of disconnected youth had parents who had some schooling beyond high school, compared to half (50.9%) of the parents of their connected counterparts. Among dual-parent households, slightly more than one quarter of disconnected youth had both parents with some education beyond high school, compared to about 46% of their connected counterparts.

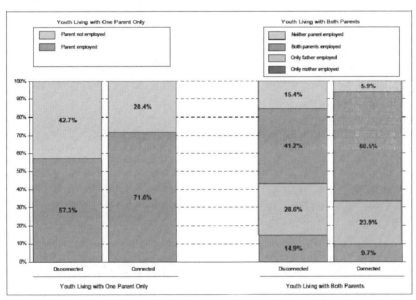

Source: Congressional Research Service based on analysis of data from the U.S. Census Bureau 2011 Current Population Survey (CPS) Annual Social and Economic Supplement (ASEC). See Table B-12 in Appendix B for greater detail.

Notes: Disconnected youth are youth who were not working or in school at the time of the survey and were reported as having not worked during the previous year for reasons other than going to school.

Figure 11. Employment Status of Disconnected and Connected Youths' Parents, for Youth Ages 16-24 Living with One or Both Parents, 2011.

The employment status of parents was also evaluated. **Figure 11** shows employment status among parents of disconnected and connected youth by household type. Among youth living in single-parent households, disconnected youth were more likely to have parents who were not employed (42.7%) at the time of the survey than connected youth (28.4%). Among youth living in dual-parent households, the divide was even greater: for 15.4% of disconnected youth, both parents were not employed at the time of the survey, compared to 5.9% of connected youth.

Differences in parents' characteristics may account in part for disconnected youths' higher poverty rates when compared to their connected counterparts, as seen earlier in **Figure 9.** Disconnected youth are not only more likely than their connected peers to live in single-parent families, who tend to have higher poverty rates than dual-parent families, but in each family type their parents are less likely to have completed high school, or to have continued their education beyond high school, and their parents are less likely to be employed, as seen above in **Figure 10** and **Figure 11**. Youths' family living arrangements, parental characteristics, and poverty status may all contribute to whether a youth becomes disconnected, or stays connected, in making the transition from adolescence to adulthood. These issues in the context of other research are discussed further in this report's conclusion.

Trends over Time

Turning now to trends over time, rates of disconnection among youth ages 16 through 24 for over the past 24 years (1988 through 2011) are presented in this section. The overall rate of disconnection, 6.9% in 2011, was higher than the 4.8% rate of 1988, the first year depicted in **Figure 12**, below. In the intervening years there was considerable variation in the overall rate, ranging from a high of 7.4% in 2010 to a low of 3.9% in 1999. The data series shows distinctive inflection points, in which disconnection rates reach local peaks, or troughs. Over four periods, rates of disconnection have shown to have been falling (1988-1990, 1994-1999, 2005-2008, 2010-2011), and in three periods to have been rising (1990-1994, 1999-2005, and 2007-2010). Although the rates of disconnection were lower in 2011 than in 2010, it is not yet clear whether a downward trend will emerge.

The local minimums in 1990 (4.1%), 1999 (3.9%) and 2007 (4.9%) temporally occur just prior to or contemporaneous with the onset of periods of economic recession (July 1990 to March 1991, March 2001 to November 2001, and December 2007 to March 2009). The local maximums in 1994 (6.6%), 2005 (5.2%), and 2010 (7.4%) are not reached until several years past the end of economic recession. The trends show that disconnected rates follow economic cycles, which should be expected, as disconnection is tied, by definition, to not being employed. Unemployment tends to be a lagging economic indicator, usually peaking for the population as a whole well past the end of economic recessions.

Gender

Figure 12 shows that the trends in disconnection rates for males and females for the most part ran parallel to each other, with disconnection rates for females consistently higher than those for males over the period. The differences are larger in earlier years (as much as 3.3 percentage points in 1990) than in later years (as little as 0.1 percentage points in 2010). Disconnection rates for females peaked in 1994, at 8.2%, and for males, at 7.4% in 2010. As noted earlier, single parenthood is a contributing factor to higher rates of disconnection among females than males. The presence of a child could make connections to work or school for these women tenuous. Trends in the effects of parenthood on disconnectedness will be addressed in greater detail later in this report, where **Figures 17** through **19** are discussed. One other note relating to **Figure 12** is that where trends in disconnection rates among males and females generally ran parallel to each other over the period depicted, from 2005 to 2008 they diverged from one another. From 2005 to 2008 disconnection rates among females rose by 0.7 percentage point, whereas among males they fell by 1.0 percentage point. Rates of disconnection increased for both males and females to 7.4% and 7.5%, respectively, in 2010; however, rates of disconnection diverged again in 2011, with males at 6.4% and females at 7.4%. CRS does not have an explanation for this divergence in rates by gender in the past three years, but possible contributing factors will be highlighted as the presentation unfolds below.

Age and Gender

CRS examined disconnection over time by gender across age groups—16 through 18, 19 through 21, and 22 through 24. **Figure 13** and **Figure 14** display these data for males and females, respectively. The figures show that disconnection rates were consistently lower for male and female youth ages 16 through 18 than among their older counterparts. For males (**Figure 13**) disconnection rates for 19-through 21-year olds tended to be slightly above those of 22-through 24-year olds over the past decade. For females (**Figure 14**), there was no distinct difference between the two oldest age groups from 1998 through 2002; however, beginning with 2003, rates of disconnection trended somewhat above their slightly younger counterparts. Disconnection rates for both males and females in each age group depict some of the cyclical patterns that were associated in the earlier discussion with general economic conditions. The trend in the youngest age group shows less cyclical variation than the older groups, as school tends to harbor the youngest group even in hard economic times, whereas older youth are subject more to labor market conditions. Females in the oldest group, ages 22 through 24, showed marked increases in their disconnection rates from 1999 to 2011, with disconnection rates more than doubling over the period, from 4.6% to 10.2%, respectively (**Figure 14**). Females ages 19 through 21 saw their disconnection rate increase by almost four full percentages points from a historic low of 5.7% in 2004, to 9.6% in 2010 (**Figure 14**).

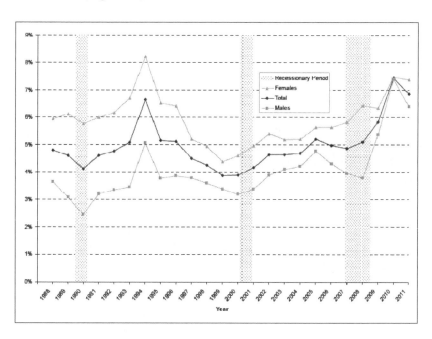

Figure 12. Rates of Disconnected Youth Ages16-24, by Gender, 1988-2011.

Race, Ethnicity, and Gender

As shown in **Table 1**, earlier, minorities are overrepresented among the disconnected youth population. Perhaps most striking is the percentage of black (non-Hispanic) males who are disconnected relative to their white (non-Hispanic) and Hispanic counterparts (see **Figure 15**). Over the period depicted, the disconnected rate for black males averaged 6.6 percentage points above that of their white non-Hispanic counterparts, and 4.7 percentage points above that of Hispanic males. The gap was largest in 2003 when the disconnection rate of black males reached a historic high of 12.4%, which was 9.8 percentage points above their white counterparts (2.6%), and 8.9 percentage points above that of male Hispanic youth (3.5%). In that year, black males were nearly five times more likely to be disconnected than white males, and three and one-half times more likely than Hispanic males. Black male youth experienced a drop in their disconnection rate, with the rate being nearly cut in half, from 12.4% in 2003 to 6.8% in 200. The rate of disconnection increased again in 2009 and 2010—and then decreased slightly in 2011.

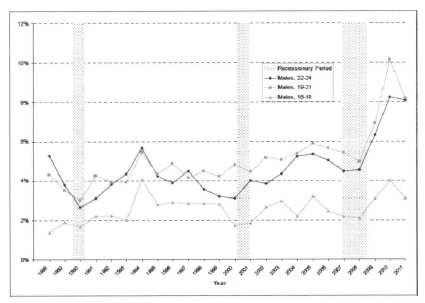

Source: Congressional Research Service based on analysis of data from the U.S. Census Bureau 1988 through 2011 Current Population Survey (CPS) Annual Social and Economic Supplement (ASEC). See Table C-2 in Appendix C for greater detail.

Notes: Disconnected youth are youth who were not working or in school at the time of the survey and were reported as having not worked during the previous year for reasons other than going to school.

Figure 13. Rates of Disconnected Males Ages 16-24, by Age Group, 1988-2011.

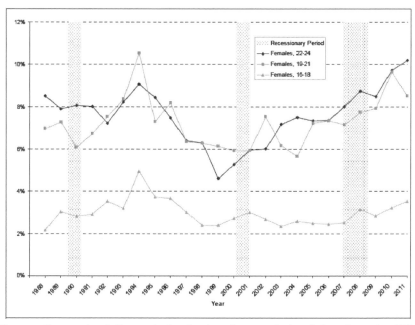

Source: Congressional Research Service based on analysis of data from the U.S.
    Census Bureau 1988 through 2011 Current Population Survey (CPS) Annual
    Social and Economic Supplement (ASEC). See Table C-3 in Appendix C for
    greater detail.
Notes: Disconnected youth are youth who were not working or in school at the time of
    the survey and were reported as having not worked during the previous year for
    reasons other than going to school.

Figure 14. Rates of Disconnected Females Ages 16-24, by Age Group, 2011.

Turning to females, **Figure 16** shows marked differences in the level and
trend in disconnection rates among white (non-Hispanic), black (non-
Hispanic), and Hispanic females over the 1988 through 2011 period.
Disconnection rates for black (non-Hispanic) and Hispanic females were
consistently higher than those of their white (non-Hispanic) counterparts.
However, while black and Hispanic females experienced substantial
reductions in their rates of disconnection from their peak rates, the rate of
disconnection among white females steadily increased since 2000. **Figure 16**
shows that among black females, their disconnection rate fell from a high of
15.1% in 1993 to a low of 6.3% in 1999—a near 60% reduction; for Hispanic
females, their rate fell from a high of 15.7% in 1994 to a low of 8.4% in

2004—a 47% reduction. The white females' disconnection rate fell from a high of 5.6% in 1994 to a low of 2.7% in 2000, but increased in each succeeding year. In 2011, the rate of disconnection among white females was at its highest point—5.9%. Still, disconnection rates increased for black and Hispanic females in recent years, with black females experiencing the largest increase, seeing their disconnection rate rise from 6.3% in 1999 to 10.5% in 2011.

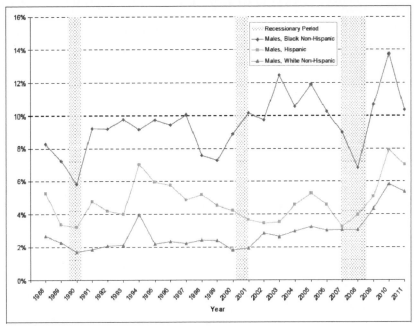

Source: Congressional Research Service based on analysis of data from the U.S. Census Bureau 1988 through 2011 Current Population Survey (CPS) Annual Social and Economic Supplement (ASEC). See Table C-4 in Appendix C for greater detail.

Notes: Disconnected youth are youth who were not working or in school at the time of the survey and were reported as having not worked during the previous year for reasons other than going to school.

Figure 15. Rates of Disconnected Males Ages 16-24, by Race and Ethnicity, 1998-2011.

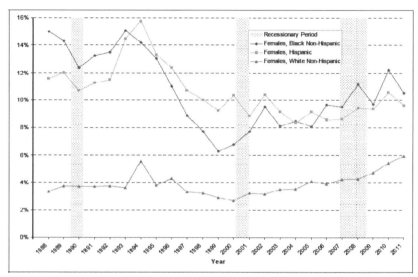

Source: Congressional Research Service based on analysis of data from the U.S.
    Census Bureau 1988 through 2011 Current Population Survey (CPS) Annual
    Social and Economic Supplement (ASEC). See Table C-5 in Appendix C for
    greater detail.
Notes: Disconnected youth are youth who were not working or in school at the time of
    the survey and were reported as having not worked during the previous year for
    reasons other than going to school.

Figure 16. Rates of Disconnected Females Ages 16-24, by Race and Ethnicity, 1998-
2011.

Figure 17, **Figure 18**, and **Figure 19** provide breakouts for each of the
three female groups respectively (white non-Hispanics, black non-Hispanics,
and Hispanics) in greater detail, depicting the effects of having a child on
disconnection rates. For purposes of historical comparison, the method of
identifying youth who are parents over the 1988 through 2011 period differs
from that used in the 2011 cross-sectional data presented earlier (**Figure 1**,
Figure 2, and **Figure 3**).[53] The changes in childbearing on female youth
disconnectedness is striking for all three groups. **Figure 17**, **Figure 18**, and
Figure 19 highlight that disconnection rates among females declined
significantly over the mid- to late 1990s for white and black non-Hispanic, as
well as Hispanic, females. While favorable economic conditions over the
period likely contributed to declines in their rates of disconnection, significant
reductions in disconnection rates appear to have occurred as a result of

declines in the share of females with children, most of whom were single parents, over the period. Black female youth in particular experienced remarkable reductions in disconnection, due in large part to reductions in childbearing. **Figure 18** shows, for example, that in 1993, the peak year of black female disconnection, a total of 15.1% were disconnected; having a child likely contributed to attaining that status for 11.3% of the population, and other factors contributed for the remaining 3.8%. By 1999, the year with the lowest proportion of disconnected black female youth, 6.3% were disconnected. Their *base rate* of disconnection among those not having a child was 3.4%, just slightly below the 1993 *base rate*, but the rate for those having a child was just 2.9%, or about one-quarter of what it was in 1993. By 2011, the *base rate* of disconnectedness among black females (6.5%) was about the same as the *total rate* of disconnectedness in 1999, but adding an additional 4.0% of youth who had a child and were disconnected raises the *total rate* of disconnected black female youth to 10.5% in 2011.

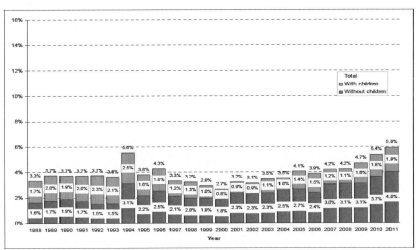

Source: Congressional Research Service based on analysis of data from the U.S. Census Bureau 1988 through 2011 Current Population Survey (CPS) Annual Social and Economic Supplement (ASEC). See Table C-6 in Appendix C for greater detail.

Notes: Disconnected youth are youth who were not working or in school at the time of the survey and were reported as having not worked during the previous year for reasons other than going to school.

Figure 17. Rates of Disconnected White, non-Hispanic Females Ages 16-24, by Parental Status, 1988-2011.

Although the share of females with children has declined since the mid-1990s, **Figure 17** shows that rates of parenting among disconnected white females began to increase in 2001, and they nearly equaled earlier peak levels by 2011. In 2001, the *base rate* of disconnectedness among white females was 1.8% and the rate for those having a child was 0.9%. These figures doubled to 4.0% and 1.9%, respectively, by 2011, when white females experienced their highest rate of disconnection at 5.9%.

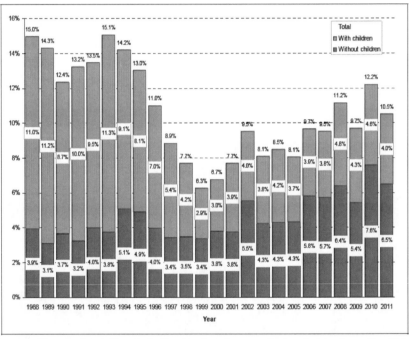

Source: Congressional Research Service based on analysis of data from the U.S. Census Bureau 1988 through 2011 Current Population Survey (CPS) Annual Social and Economic Supplement (ASEC). See Table C-6 in Appendix C for greater detail.

Notes: Disconnected youth are youth who were not working or in school at the time of the survey and were reported as having not worked during the previous year for reasons other than going to school.

Figure 18. Rates of Disconnected Black, non-Hispanic Females Ages 16-24, by Parental Status,1988-2011.

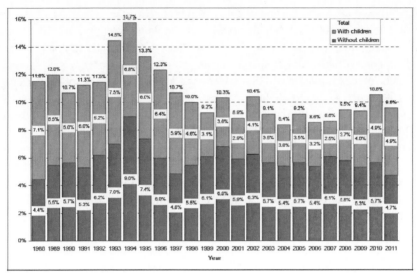

Source: Congressional Research Service based on analysis of data from the U.S.
    Census Bureau 1988 through 2011 Current Population Survey (CPS) Annual
    Social and Economic Supplement (ASEC). See Table C-6 in Appendix C for
    greater detail.
Notes: Disconnected youth are youth who were not working or in school at the time of
    the survey and were reported as having not worked during the previous year for
    reasons other than going to school.

Figure 19. Rates of Disconnected Hispanic Females Ages 16-24, by Parental
Status,1988-2011.

Figure 20 addresses the question of whether the decline in female
disconnection relating to parenting was the result of a reduced tendency for
females age 16 through 24 to be single parents, or whether, among single
mothers, there was a greater tendency for them to be connected, rather than
disconnected, in more recent years. **Figure 20** presents data in two columns.
The first column shows the percent of females age 16 through 24 who were
single parents over the 1988 through 2011 period, by race and ethnicity,
addressing the first question posed above. The second column shows the
composition of single mothers, by whether they were connected or
disconnected, addressing the second question posed above.

As for the first question, the figure shows that the rates of single
parenthood remained stable or decreased among the three racial/ethnic groups
over the 1988 through 2011 period, and that these rates have varied across
groups (first column). The figure shows that black females age 16 through 24

have shown a marked decline in single parenting over the period. In 1989, for example, 29.9% of black female youth were single parents; by 2011, the share that were single parents fell to 17.4%, nearly a 42% decline. In contrast, for white non-Hispanic and Hispanic female youth, the share who were single parents increased over the 1988 to 1997 period, reaching a peak for each group in 1997, and decreased slightly in most years thereafter. Among white non-Hispanic female youth, the share who were single parents rose from 5.2% in 1988, to a high of 8.1% in 1997 (a 56% increase), and fell slightly to 7.9% in the first quarter of 2011. Among Hispanic female youth the share who were single parents rose from 10.4% in 1989 to a peak of 15.9% in 1997 (a 53% increase). In 2011, the rate was 14.6%. Now, turning to the second question, the second column of **Figure 20** shows single mothers by whether they were connected to work or school, or disconnected from both, over the 1988 through 2011 period. First, all three panels show that youth who are single mothers were more likely to be connected than they were to be disconnected. This holds true over the entire 24-year time frame, and for each of the three racial/ethnic groups presented, with the exception of Hispanic single mothers in 1989 and 1994, where they were about equally likely to be connected as to be disconnected. All three panels show a marked increase in the connection rate among single female parents from the 1993-1994 through 1999-2001 period. Among white non-Hispanic youth who were single mothers, the share that was connected to school or work increased over the 1994 to 2001 period, from 75% in 1993 to 90% in 2001. Among black non-Hispanic youth who were single mothers, the share that was connected to school or work increased over the 1993 to 2000 period, from about 62% in 1993 to 90% in 2000. It is worth pointing out that in 2000, black single mothers were as likely to be connected to work or school as their white non-Hispanic counterparts. From 1994 through 1999, the share of Hispanic single mothers who were connected to work or school increased from just under 50% to 79%. Single Hispanic mothers' rates of connection to work or school consistently are below those of their white and black non-Hispanic counterparts. From 2000 through 2011, attachment to school or work of single mothers in all three racial/ethnic groups declined, but the level of attachment was still well above what it was in the late 1980s and early 1990s. No clear trend in Hispanic single mothers' connection rates is discernable in the post-2000 period, as their connection rates vacillated; however, in 2010 and 2011, their rates of connectedness were at their lowest points over the period.

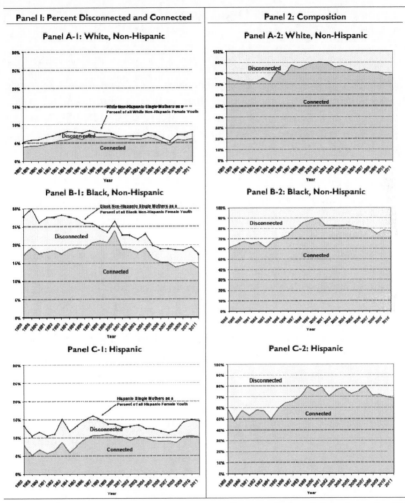

Source: Congressional Research Service Based on analysis of data from the U.S.
    Census Bureau 1988 through 2011 Current Population Survey (CPS Annual
    Social and Economic Supplement (ASEC). See Table C-7 in Appendix C for
    greater detail.
Notes: Disconnected youth are youth who were not working or in school at the time of
    the survey and were reported as having not worked during the previous year for
    reasons other than going to school.

Figure 20. Single Mothers as a Percent of All Female Youth Ages 16-24 and
Composition of Single Mothers by Connected and Disconnected Status, by Race and
Ethnicity, 1988-2011.

DISCUSSION

Overview

The CRS analysis shows that disconnected youth are more likely to be female, black or Hispanic, and in their early- to mid-twenties. It also demonstrates that disconnected youth are a diverse group. Disability appears to be at least part of the reason some youth are not working or in school (Figure 1). Nearly 30% of all youth reported they were not working because they were disabled, of whom just over 40% had a disability severe enough that they received SSI or Medicare.

About another 30% reported having childrearing and homemaking responsibilities that kept them from work, while the remaining youth did not have disabilities or child and home-related responsibilities. These home-related responsibilities could include caring for siblings or managing a household because their parents have a disability or some other reason.

Among females, those who were parenting were well represented among the disconnected youth population, although rates of disconnection have decreased over time for single mothers (Figures 17 through 20). It is unclear to what extent having a disability, caring for a child, or having responsibilities in the home actually keeps youth from engaging in school or work.

Some may respond to CPS questions in what they believe to be a socially appropriate manner, and they may recognize that being idle is not widely acceptable.

Still, one third of youth (or their parents) reported that they (the youth) did not have any limitations that would keep them from work. These youth could be considered the "hard core" of the disconnected. Yet even they may have "legitimate" limitations that are keeping them idle, such as an undiagnosed disability.

Future research is needed to better understand the reasons youth are disconnected, and whether these reasons are legitimately keeping youth from attending school or working.

Disconnected youth will likely face numerous challenges as they transition to adulthood. In terms of education, these youth are foregoing an opportunity to attain a high school diploma or GED, or additional years of schooling that can assist them in securing employment and gaining experience that will contribute to future employability.

About three out of ten disconnected youth ages 19 through 24 lack a high school diploma or its equivalent (Figure 4).

For these youth in particular, securing stable, well-paying employment may be unlikely, particularly in the current economic climate. Being out of the labor force—especially for an extended period—can have lasting effects for disconnected youth.

Without an adequate employment history, disconnected youth may lack access to health insurance. Nearly four out of ten disconnected youth are uninsured (Figure 7).

Another consequence of being out of the workforce is foregone current wages and future higher wages that are commensurate with work experience. Somewhat less than half of all disconnected youth are poor (Figure 5, and discussed in further detail below), and even having additional education beyond high school does not mitigate their relatively high levels of poverty when compared to their connected peers (Figure 6).

Additional research is needed to better understand how poor disconnected youth are making ends meet. Surely some of them receive assistance through informal networks in the form of providing child care, work in the informal economy, and temporary housing.

And many are likely eligible for federal cash and non-cash assistance programs, including public housing. Yet because the CPS is limited to surveying individuals in households, the analysis in this report does not capture those who are homeless or are in jails, prisons, or residential treatment facilities. If these groups were surveyed, rates of disconnection would likely be higher.

The CPS similarly does not include youth who might offset rates of disconnection, such as those youth residing in college dorms and on military bases. At least a few studies have attempted to factor in imprisoned and active military populations, but additional work is needed to incorporate other groups of youth.

The CRS analysis expands the current research by examining the characteristics of disconnected youths' parents. Because the CPS is a cross-sectional data set, CRS could not evaluate antecedent conditions or events affecting youth or their parents that may contribute to later youth disconnection.

However, the analysis in this report hints that disconnection may be intergenerational, meaning that the parents of youth who are currently disconnected could have experienced periods in which they were not working or in school.

In fact, a significant share of parents of disconnected youth were not working at the time of the 2011 survey (Figure 11). Among disconnected youth living in single-parent households, over 40% had parents who were not employed.

Additionally, disconnected youths' co-residing parents were more likely to lack a high school diploma or its equivalent compared to connected youths' co-residing parents (Figure 10).

The next section further examines the role of family characteristics and other related factors that likely influence disconnectedness.

Poverty, Family Living Arrangements, and Parental Characteristics

Given CRS' findings and the discussion which follows, the connections between poverty, family background, living arrangements and youth disconnectedness are interrelated.

In some cases, disconnectedness may be a cause for high poverty rates among such youth, especially among those who are living apart from family or other relatives.

Among youth living apart from parents, the poverty rate of disconnected youth (71.6%) was twice that of connected youth (34.6%) (**Figure 9**). In other cases, poverty may contribute to youth becoming disconnected. Here the connection is more complex.

CRS found that disconnected youth, even when living with both their parents, were almost three times more likely to be poor than connected youth, 17.4% compared to 6.2%, respectively, and when living with only one parent, twice as likely to be poor than their connected counterparts, 47.4% compared to 24.5%. When living with a parent, disconnected youth were about as likely to live with only one parent (29.4%) than with both parents (29.1%), whereas connected youth were more likely to live with both parents (46.6%) than just one (22.5%) (**Figure 8**).

When parents' characteristics are examined, disconnected youth were about twice as likely to have parents who had not completed high school than were connected youth (**Figure 10**); for disconnected youth in single-parent families, 25.6% had a parent who had not completed high school, compared to 15.5% of connected youth; for youth living in families with both parents, 31.7% had either one or both parents not having attained a high school diploma or its equivalent, compared to 16.5% of connected youth. Furthermore, disconnected youth were more likely to have a parent who was not working at the time of the survey (**Figure 11**).

Among disconnected youth living with only one parent, the share with a nonworking parent (42.7%) was greater than that of connected youth (28.4%); among disconnected youth living with both parents, the share of disconnected youth where both parents were not working (15.4%) was almost three times that of connected youth (5.9%).

Research evidence indicates that living in poverty has negative effects on children's life outcomes that may range well into adulthood. By almost any indicator, poor children fare worse than their non-poor counterparts. Poor children tend to score lower on standardized tests of IQ, verbal ability, and achievement, and are less likely to advance in grade and complete high school. Poor teen adolescent girls are more likely to become teenage mothers than their non-poor counterparts, contributing to a cycle of poverty from one generation to the next.

While income poverty is associated with poor child outcomes, lack of income in itself may account for only part of the reason why poor children face poor future prospects. Other factors, such as a safe and nurturing home environment, and parental characteristics associated with their income, are arguably as important, if not more so, than income, per se, in affecting children's life chances.[54]

The research evidence indicates that poverty's lasting effects are most dramatic for children who experience persistent and/or deep poverty when they are younger.

Among adolescents, the evidence of poverty's negative effects on outcomes is much less clear. For example, poverty among adolescents is negatively related to high school graduation, college attendance, and years of schooling.

The U.S. Department of Education reports high school dropout rates for a cohort of 10th through 12th graders in the early 1990s were almost 3 times higher for students living in poor families (10.9%) than for children living in families with incomes above poverty (3.6%).[55]

Other researchers using NLSY79 data found that children who spent one to three years of their adolescence in poverty were 60% less likely to graduate from high school than those who were not poor, and those who spent four years of adolescence in poverty were 75% less likely. [56]

Respectively, children who spent part or all of their adolescence in poverty were 40% and 60% less likely to attend college than other children, and on average attained between 1.0 and 1.75 fewer years of education.

While the evidence presented above suggests a strong relationship between adolescent poverty and educational attainment, the NLSY researchers most importantly found that the relationship withers when other control variables, such as parental education, family structure, and IQ are taken into account.

The researchers found that *"after the control variables were taken into account, the number of years spent below the poverty line during adolescence were not related to any of the educational outcomes considered" (emphasis added).*[57]

Yet when viewed over a longer period of time than just adolescence, growing up in poverty does appear to have an effect on educational attainment, even after controlling for other background factors. Researchers using 21 years of Panel Study of Income Dynamics (PSID) data found that all other things being equal, the number of years that children spend in poverty while growing up is an important factor in predicting whether they will graduate from high school.[58] These researchers found that growing up with a single parent further reduces the probability of high school completion.

These researchers also examined the effects of poverty on teen non-marital births. They found that parental characteristics (such as mother's education) and the number of years spent living with a single parent had a significant effect on the probability that as a teen a girl would have a non-marital birth, and that poverty, in itself, was not a significant factor.[59] As shown earlier, in **Figure 1**, about one-in-six disconnected youth have a child, most of whom are unmarried women.

The same factors affecting school achievement and teen non-marital births are likely to have a similar bearing on youth disconnectedness. Family background characteristics over the course of a child's lifetime are likely to affect the chances that youth become disconnected in making the transition from adolescence into adulthood.

The analysis for this report, however, only describes differences between disconnected and connected youth at a point in time rather than over their life-course. The cross-sectional snapshot presented in this report only hints at possible differences that disconnected and connected youth may have experienced over the course of their childhood.

Implications for Policy

The time trend data presented show little difference in the overall rate of disconnection among youth in 2011 compared to 23 years earlier, in 1988. However, over the period, there was considerable variation in the overall rate and in disconnection rates among and between racial and ethnic groups, by gender, although disconnection among all single parenting females has declined since the mid-1990s, particularly for young black women. The trend data show that youth disconnection follows economic cycles, as should be expected.

During recessions, when jobs in the economy become scarce, rates of youth disconnection increase; during periods of economic expansion, rates of youth disconnection decrease. The data presented in this report end during 2010 and the first part of 2011 (i.e., February through April), two years after the end of the most recent recession.

In addition to overall economic conditions, a number of other factors may contribute to changes in the rates of disconnection. For example, the following factors may have lent to the decreasing rates of disconnection, particularly among black single mothers, since the mid-1990s: an expansion of the Earned Income Tax Credit (EITC), phased in between 1994 and 1996; welfare reform in 1996, which introduced time limits and work requirements for families receiving benefits and services under the newly enacted Temporary Assistance for Needy Families (TANF) block grant; and declining teen birth rates, beginning in approximately 1992.

Clearly, given the state of the current economy, youth disconnection rates would be expected to stabilize. For females, their overall disconnection rate will depend not only on the *base rate*, depicted as the rate of disconnection among females without children as a percent of all females, and the additional rate of disconnection tied to having a child and not being married to a connected husband.

The rate of disconnection among females who are not parents has been on the rise in recent years. Given the large declines in the rate of disconnection among females since the early 1990s relating to childbearing, their overall rate of disconnection in near-future years may not reach the levels seen in the early 1990s and preceding years.

Overall, young single mothers are more likely to be connected to school or work than to be disconnected from both. Moreover, from the early- to mid-1990s to around 2000, the likelihood of younger single mothers being connected to work or school increased, and their rate of disconnection decreased. Since then their rate of disconnection has increased, but not yet to the levels seen in the late 1980s and early 1990s.

Being connected to work or school is important for both youth and greater society. As discussed above, the individual costs of disconnection are great. While out of school or work, youth forego gaining experience that can lead to better employment opportunities. They are also more likely to live in poverty and lack health insurance.

Further, the young children of disconnected youth are at risk of growing up in poverty, which as discussed above, can have far reaching consequences in adulthood. The costs to society may also be great, though little research has been done in this area.

Youth who are disconnected may pose a financial burden if they rely on cash and non-cash assistance programs, or if they become homeless.

Perhaps more importantly, in an increasingly global economy and with retirement underway for Baby Boomers, society has a strong interest in ensuring that all young people today have the educational attainment and employment experience to become skilled workers, contributing taxpayers, and participants in civic life.

Interventions to connect youth to school and work depend on a number of factors. The research literature has devoted attention to the *timing* of interventions.

The timing can target early childhood, the elementary and middle school years, or the high school years and just beyond. During each of these phases, developmental outcomes are influenced by a myriad of environmental and social factors, including family structure, stability, and functioning; economic circumstances; education; health care; and schooling.[60]

They are also influenced by innate and inherited characteristics. These factors can influence how well youth ultimately make the transition to adulthood. The research literature has identified certain markers of risk and problem behaviors in the middle and older youth years that are associated with later negative outcomes.[61]

Markers of risk suggest that youth will likely experience poor outcomes in adolescence and beyond. These markers are tangible indicators that can be measured or documented, and include low school performance and involvement in the child welfare system.

Problem behaviors are activities that have the potential to hurt youth, the community, or both. Behaviors include early sexual experimentation; truancy; use of tobacco, alcohol, or other drugs; running away from home or foster care; and association with delinquent peers.

James Heckman and others assert that investments in early childhood can, in part, serve as a protective factor against poor outcomes, especially when coupled with investments during the elementary school years.[62]

Other research has focused on the benefits of intervening at an older age when young people are at risk of or are already experiencing negative outcomes.[63] And still other research has begun to examine the effects of a system of interventions that targets youth throughout their early life, from the infant years to young adulthood.[64]

Youth might benefit from interventions during all stages of their early life, particularly if they begin to exhibit markers of risk such as low school performance.

Interventions can also focus on particular *institutions or systems*, such as the family, community, schools, and job training programs. These interventions may help to address some of the reasons why youth are not working or in school. First, interventions in the family at all stages could benefit disconnected youth.[65]

Many of the disconnected youth in the analysis are parenting. Adequate child care may be one way in which to assist these youth in becoming connected to school or work and remain connected.

Further, given the possibility that disconnection is intergenerational, early parenting classes or home-based interventions could provide a buffer for the children of disconnected youth from experiencing negative outcomes later in their lives. In the community, interventions could focus on assisting youth with disabilities since they make up a large share of the disconnected youth population.

Such supportive services might include mental health care. Young disconnected single mothers could benefit from the involvement of their children's fathers. Responsible fatherhood programs seek to engage fathers in assisting with childrearing and child support, which may in turn enable mothers to secure child care and other assistance so they can work or attend school. Other community interventions could involve programs that encourage young women to delay childbearing, as parenting appears to be strongly associated with disconnection among females.

Finally, school and job training programs that provide wraparound services—counseling, child care, transportation, assistance with attaining a high school diploma, and preparation for the workforce—may help to reengage youth.

A number of interventions have been designed in recent years that seek to address multiple aspects of a youth's circumstances.[66] In addition, sexual education in schools may help to encourage sexual avoidance and teen pregnancy.[67] However, as shown in this report, disconnected youth make up a diverse group and no one intervention is likely to be a panacea.

APPENDIX A. SUMMARY OF MAJOR STUDIES ON DISCONNECTED YOUTH

Table A-1. Select Studies of Disconnected Youth

Study and Data Set	Definition(s) of Disconnected Youth	Number and/or Percentage of Disconnected Youth (by gender, race, and ethnicity, if applicable)	Other Information on Disconnected Youth
The Condition of Education (2007), U.S. Department of Education, National Center for Education Statistics. Current Population Survey, Census Bureau, U.S. Department of Commerce.	Disconnected label not applied; however, the study evaluated the number and characteristics of non-institutionalized youth 16 through 19 who were out of school and not working. The study appears to be a point-in-time estimate. The study does not specify the length of time these youth are not working or in school.	In 2006, 7.6% of youth met the definition of youth who were not in school or working. From 1986 through 2006, the percentage of these youth ranged from a low of 7.2% in 2004 to a high of 10.0% in 1992. Disconnected youth by gender in 2006: males - 7.1% females - 8.1% Disconnected youth by race and ethnicity in 2006: white - 5.9% black - 11.5% Hispanic - 10.6% Asian and Pacific Islander - 5.7%	In 2006, of U.S.-born youth, 7.2% were disconnected; of naturalized U.S. citizens, 8.3% were disconnected; and of youth who are non-citizens, 13.5% were disconnected.
		Youth ages 16 through 19 who met the definition of youth who were not working or in school, by gender in 2000 (and if institutionalized youth and members of the armed forces are counted):	Teens from low-income families are more likely to be neither enrolled in school nor employed than those from higher-income families. Teens whose parents did not finish high school are twice as likely to be neither working nor in school as those whose parents have at least some education (actual statistics not provided).

Study and Data Set	Definition(s) of Disconnected Youth	Number and/or Percentage of Disconnected Youth (by gender, race, and ethnicity, if applicable)	Other Information on Disconnected Youth
What is Happening to Youth Employment Rates? (2004), *Congressional Budget Office.* Current Population Survey, Census Bureau, U.S. Department of Commerce.	Disconnected label not applied; however, the study evaluated the number and characteristics of non-institutionalized and institutionalized youth ages 16 through 24 who were out of school and not working.	males – 8% (10%) females - 9% (9%) Youth ages 20 through 24 who met the definition of disconnected, by gender in 2000 (and if institutionalized youth and members of the armed forces are counted): males – 11% (13%) females - 18% (18%) During the months of the school year in 2000, an average of four million youth ages 16 through 24 were neither in school nor working, of whom 60% were female. Nearly 40% of those youth had not finished high school, and most were not looking for work.	
Kids Count (20!!), *Annie E. Casey Foundation.* American Community Survey, Census Bureau, U.S. Department of Commerce.	The disconnected label applies to non-institutionalized youth ages 16 to 19 who are not currently working or in school. The disconnected youth label also applies to non-institutionalized young adults 18 to 24 who are currently not working or in school, and have no degree beyond a high school diploma or GED.	In 2010, 1.6 million (8.0%) youth ages 16 to 19 met the definition of disconnected. From 2002 through 2006, the percentage of disconnected youth ages 16 to 19 ranged from 8.0% to 9.0%. Disconnected youth ages 16 to 19 by race and ethnicity in 2009 (2010 not available): white non-Hispanic -7.0% black non-Hispanic - 13.0% American Indian and Alaska Native non-Hispanic - 17.0% Hispanic - 12.0%	In 2010, Nevada had the highest share of disconnected youth ages 16 through 19 (15%) and Connecticut had the lowest (4%). In 2009, Nevada had the highest share of disconnected youth ages 18 through 24 (22%) and North Dakota had the lowest (8%).

Table A-1. (Continued)

Study and Data Set	Definition(s) of Disconnected Youth	Number and/or Percentage of Disconnected Youth (by gender, race, and ethnicity, if applicable)	Other Information on Disconnected Youth
		Asian and Pacific Islander non-Hispanic – 5.0% In 2009, 4.3 million (16.0%) youth ages 18 to 24 met the definition of disconnected. In each year from 2002 through 2009, 15% to 16% of youth ages 18 to 24 met the definition of disconnected.	
Reconnecting Disadvantaged Young Men (2006), by Peter Edelman, Harry J. Holzer, and Paul Offner. Current Population Survey, Census Bureau, U.S. Department of Commerce. Supplemented with data on youth incarceration rates from the Bureau of Justice Statistics, U.S. Department of Justice.	Disconnected youth label applies to both incarcerated and non-incarcerated youth ages 16 through 24 who are not working or in school for at least a year. Both incarcerated and non-incarcerated youth ages 16 through 24 are considered "idle" if they not working or in school for less than one year.	Percentages of disconnected youth in 1999 by race, gender and ethnicity (and if incarcerated youth are counted): Disconnected youth: white males – 3.2% (4.2%) black males – 10.5% (17.1%) Hispanic males – 9.3% (11.9%) white females – 7.1% (7.1%) *No difference* black females – 9.0% (9.9%) Hispanic females – 10.4% (10.4%) *No difference*	White youth ages 16 to 24 are more likely than their black and Hispanic counterparts to be enrolled in secondary, post-secondary, or other school. Among youth who are working, but not in school, white youth are also more likely to be employed.
		Idle youth: white males – 8.7% (9.6%) black males – 22.8% (28.5%) Hispanic males – 12.8% (15.3%) white females – 13.3% (13.3%) *No difference* black females – 21.6% (22.4%)	

Study and Data Set	Definition(s) of Disconnected Youth	Number and/or Percentage of Disconnected Youth (by gender, race, and ethnicity, if applicable)	Other Information on Disconnected Youth
Left Behind in the Labor Market: Labor Market Problems of the Nation's Out-of-School, Young Adult Populations (2003), by Andrew Sum et al., Northeastern University. Current Population Survey, Census Bureau, U.S. Department of Commerce.	Disconnected label not applied; however, the study evaluated the number and characteristics of non-institutionalized youth ages 16 through 24 who were out of school and not working. The estimates are annual averages based on the monthly CPS survey.	Hispanic females – 28.8% (28.8%) *No difference* In 2001, 5.2 million youth ages 16 to 24 (14.8%) were not in school or working. About 44% dropped out of high school. In 2001, approximately 2.2. million men (12.6% of the 16-through 24- year old male population) and 3.0 million women (17.0% of the 16- through 24-year old female population) were not working or in school. In select years from 1989 through 2001, the percentage of disconnected youth who were not in school or working has ranged from a low of 14.2% in 2000 to a high of 18.5% in 1992.	About 40% of youth who were not working or in school in 2001 lived in the 50 most populous metropolitan areas. About 22% of youth who were not working or in school in 2001 were head of a non-family household, and 11% were head of a household that included non-relatives.
Prevalence, Patterns, and Outcomes, by Brett V. Brown and Carol Emig, Child Trends, in America's Disconnected Youth: Toward a Preventative Strategy, (1999), by Douglas J. Besharov, Editor. National Longitudinal Survey of Youth for 1979 (NLSY79). Youth were surveyed annually through 1994, and biennially after 1994.	Disconnected label applies to youth in the survey who were not working (including in the armed forces) or in school, and were not married to a connected spouse for at least 26 weeks in a year over the period 1979 through 1991. Short-term disconnection is 26 weeks in each of one to two years. Long-term disconnection is 26 weeks in each of three years or more.	Percentage of disconnected youth by gender, race, and ethnicity: Short-term disconnected youth: males – 24% white males – 23% black males – 28% Hispanic males – 30% females – 24% white females – 23% black females – 30% Hispanic females - 29% Long-term disconnected youth: males – 13%	About 15% of males and 22% of females who were disconnected for one to two years; and 44% of males and 56% of females who were disconnected for three or more years experienced poverty. This is compared to 3% of males and 4% of females who were not disconnected.

Table A-1. (Continued)

Study and Data Set	Definition(s) of Disconnected Youth	Number and/or Percentage of Disconnected Youth (by gender, race, and ethnicity, if applicable)	Other Information on Disconnected Youth
For purposes of the study, data were evaluated for youth who were ages 14 through 16 at the start of the survey. The most recent year for which data were evaluated was 1991, when the oldest youth in the cohort were 28.		white males – 10% black males – 26% Hispanic males – 19% females – 14% white females – 9% black females – 37% Hispanic females - 21%	Long-term disconnected youth were associated with certain personal and family background factors, including family poverty, family welfare receipt, low parent education, single/no parent family, bearing or fathering a child before age 18, dropping out of high school, and having multiple risk factors. The researchers state that these factors are interrelated and difficult to disentangle as the cause for disconnection.
Profiling the Plight of Disconnected Youth in America (2006), by Thomas MaCurdy, Bryan Keating, and Sriniketh Suryasesha Nagavarapu, Stanford University, for the William and Flora Hewlett Foundation. National Longitudinal Survey of Youth for 1997 (NLSY97). Youth are surveyed annually.	The disconnected label applies to youth in the survey who were not working or in school. A second definition applies to youth who are not in school or working, and not married. Youth are considered disconnected for a year if they were not working or in school in the month they were surveyed and in at least eight of the following eleven months over the period 1997 through 2003.	Of youth who are not in school or working: By age 20, 14.6% of youth were disconnected for at least one year and 4.6% were disconnected for at least two years. By age 22, the corresponding figures were 24.0% and 11.0%, respectively. Of youth who are not in school or working, and not married: By age 20, 12.3% were disconnected for at least one year, and 3.3% were disconnected for at least two years.	A significant share of four groups of youth had experienced disconnection by age 20: 44.9% of female youth who were mothers by age 18; 31.4% of youth were convicted of, or pled guilty to, a crime committed before age 18; 50.7% of youth who dropped out of high school; and 23.8% of youth who were not living with their parents, including foster parents, before age 18.

Study and Data Set	Definition(s) of Disconnected Youth	Number and/or Percentage of Disconnected Youth (by gender, race, and ethnicity, if applicable)	Other Information on Disconnected Youth
For purposes of the study, data were evaluated for youth who were ages 12 through 16 at the start of the survey. The most recent year for which data were evaluated was 2003, when the oldest youth in the cohort were 23.		By age 22, 19.8% were disconnected for at least one year, and 8.7% were disconnected for at least two years. Percentage of unmarried youth, by gender, race, and ethnicity, who were disconnected by age 20 (and by age 22): white males - 12.8% (19.8%) white females - 12.8% (19.8%) black males - 11.9% (35.3%) black females - 21.9% (36.6%) Hispanic males - 14.8% (25.9%) Hispanic females - 16.4% (24.1%)	No further information about these groups was provided. The probability of experiencing a disconnected episode among youth not in school or working, and not married in the survey is associated with being black and parental receipt of government aid from the time the parent was 18 (or their first child was born) until 1997. This aid includes Medicaid, Supplemental Security Income (SSI), Aid to Families with Dependent Children (replaced by Temporary Assistance to Needy Families), and food assistance.
The Transition to Adulthood: Characteristics of Young Adults Ages 18 to 24 in America (2003), by Susan Jekielek and Brett Brown, Annie E. Casey Foundation, Population Reference Bureau, and Child Trends. 2000 U.S. Census, PUMS-5 File, Census Bureau, U.S. Department of Commerce.	The disconnected label applies to non-institutionalized youth ages 18 to 24 who are not working (including in the armed forces), or in school, and have no more than a high school diploma or GED. The study appears to be a point-in-time estimate.	In 2000, the number of youth ages 18 to 24 who met the definition of disconnected was 3.8 million or 14.2% of the population. Disconnected youth ages 18 to 24 by race and ethnicity in 2000 (and share of disconnection among population): white non-Hispanic -1.6 million (9.5%) black non-Hispanic - 900,138 (24.5%) American Indian and Alaska Native non-Hispanic - 62,952 (26.3%)	Disconnected youth ages 18 to 24 by nativity in 2000 (and share of disconnection among population): Foreign born -752,918 (21.6%) Native born - 3,091,261 (13.1%) Disconnected youth by disability status (and share of disconnection among population): Disabled - 818,078 (19.6%) Not disabled - 2,729,553 (11.9%)

Table A-1. (Continued)

Study and Data Set	Definition(s) of Disconnected Youth	Number and/or Percentage of Disconnected Youth (by gender, race, and ethnicity, if applicable)	Other Information on Disconnected Youth
		Asian and Pacific Islander non-Hispanic - 70,696 (6.3%) Hispanic - 1.1 million (24.3%) Other race, non-Hispanic - 6,976 (12.9%) Two or more races, non-Hispanic - 74,720 (13.0%)	
Connected by 25: Improving the Life Chances of the Country's Most Vulnerable 14-24 Year Olds (2003), by Michael Wald and Tia Martinez, Stanford University, for the William and Flora Hewlett Foundation. Cross-sectional analyses of data from Current Population Survey, Census Bureau, U.S. Department of Commerce, and various national surveys of prison and jail populations.	The term "disconnected" is not precisely defined for youth ages 14 to 17, but youth are at risk of becoming disconnected—or having long-term spells of unemployment (i.e., one year or more)—if they are: a high school dropout; and/or in the juvenile justice system; and/or unmarried mothers; and/or in foster care. The disconnected youth label applies to youth ages 18 to 24 who have a high school degree or less and are unemployed for a year or longer, or are incarcerated.	Using data across multiple years, the number of youth ages 14 to 17 who are at risk of becoming disconnected is one million (though there may be overlap among the four categories of youth). Using data across multiple years, the number of youth ages 18 to 24 who meet the definition of disconnected is 1.8 million.	

Source: Prepared by the Congressional Research Service.

Notes: The Congressional Research Service did not evaluate the methodology or validity of the studies.

APPENDIX B. BACKGROUND TABLES FOR CONGRESSIONAL RESEARCH SERVICE ANALYSIS OF DISCONNECTED YOUTH

Table B-1. Rates of Disconnectedness Among Youth Ages 16-24, by Age Group, Gender, and Parental Status, 2011 (Numbers in 1,000s)

		Age Group		
	Total	16 - 18	19 - 21	22 - 24
All Youth	38,374	13,096	12,607	12,671
Number disconnected	2,641	434	1,053	1,155
No children	2,051	396	855	799
Has child(ren)	590	38	197	355
Disconnected rate	6.9%	3.3%	8.3%	9.1%
No children	5.3%	3.0%	6.8%	6.3%
Has child(ren)	1.5%	0.3%	1.6%	2.8%
Males				
All Male Youth	19,585	6,725	6,389	6,471
Number disconnected	1,254	209	523	523
No children	1,190	205	505	480
Has child(ren)	64	3	18	42
Disconnected rate	6.4%	3.1%	8.2%	8.1%
No children	6.1%	3.1%	7.9%	7.4%
Has child(ren)	0.3%	0.0%	0.3%	0.7%
Females				
All Female Youth	18,790	6,371	6,219	6,200
Number disconnected	1,387	226	530	632
No children	860	191	351	319
Has child(ren)	527	35	179	313
Disconnected rate	7.4%	3.5%	8.5%	10.2%
No children	4.6%	3.0%	5.6%	5.1%
Has child(ren)	2.8%	0.5%	2.9%	5.1%

Source: Congressional Research Service based on analysis of data from the U.S. Census Bureau Current Population Survey (CPS) Annual Social and Economic Supplement (ASEC). See corresponding Figure 2 in the text.

Notes: Disconnected youth are youth who were not working or in school at the time of the survey and were reported as having not worked during the previous year for reasons other than going to school.

**Table B-2. Rates of Disconnectedness Among Youth Ages 16-24,
by Race, Ethnicity, Gender, and Parental Status, 2011
(Numbers in 1,000s)**

| | | | Race and Ethnicity | | |
	Total	White, non-Hispanic	Black, non-Hispanic	Hispanic	Other, non-Hispanic
All Youth	38,374	22,638	5,438	7,573	2,726
Number disconnected	2,641	1,279	567	621	174
No children	2,051	1,035	441	431	143
Has child(ren)	590	243	126	189	32
Disconnected rate	6.9%	5.6%	10.4%	8.2%	6.4%
No children	5.3%	4.6%	8.1%	5.7%	5.2%
Has child(ren)	1.5%	1.1%	2.3%	2.5%	1.2%
Males					
All Male Youth	19,585	11,480	2,645	4,086	1,374
Number disconnected	1,254	617	274	286	78
No children	1,190	592	260	268	70
Has child(ren)	64	25	13	18	8
Disconnected rate	6.4%	5.4%	10.3%	7.0%	5.7%
No children	6.1%	5.2%	9.8%	6.6%	5.1%
Has child(ren)	0.3%	0.2%	0.5%	0.4%	0.6%
Females					
All Female Youth	18,790	11,157	2,793	3,487	1,352
Number disconnected	1,387	662	294	335	96
No children	860	443	181	164	73
Has child(ren)	527	218	113	172	24
Disconnected rate	7.4%	5.9%	10.5%	9.6%	7.1%
No children	4.6%	4.0%	6.5%	4.7%	5.4%
Has child(ren)	2.8%	2.0%	4.0%	4.9%	1.8%

Source: Congressional Research Service based on analysis of data from the U.S. Census Bureau Current Population Survey (CPS) Annual Social and Economic Supplement (ASEC). See corresponding Figure 3 in the text.

Notes: Disconnected youth are youth who were not working or in school at the time of the survey and were reported as having not worked during the previous year for reasons other than going to school. Beginning in 2003, respondents were able to report more than one race on the CPS, whereas before they could only report a single race. The data for 2011 reflect the race of respondents who reported only one race.

Table B-3. Educational Attainment of Connected and Disconnected Youth Ages 19-24, by Age Group, 2011 (Numbers in 1,000s)

	Age19 to 24		Age 19 - 21		Age 22 to 24	
	Number	Percent	Number	Percent	Number	Percent
Total Youth	25,279	100.0%	12,607	100.0%	12,671	100.0%
Lacks HS diploma	3,001	11.9%	1,758	13.9%	1,244	9.8%
HS diploma or GED	7,615	30.1%	4,089	32.4%	3,527	27.8%
Some schooling beyond HS	14,662	58.0%	6,761	53.6%	7,901	62.4%
Disconnected Youth	2,207	100.0%	1,053	100.0%	1,155	100.0%
Lacks HS diploma	669	30.3%	332	31.6%	337	29.2%
HS diploma or GED	1,102	49.9%	584	55.4%	519	44.9%
Some schooling beyond HS	436	19.8%	137	13.0%	299	25.9%
Connected Youth	23,071	100.0%	11,555	100.0%	11,517	100.0%
Lacks HS diploma	2,332	10.1%	1,425	12.3%	907	7.9%
HS diploma or GED	6,513	28.2%	3,505	30.3%	3,008	26.1%
Some schooling beyond HS	14,226	61.7%	6,624	57.3%	7,601	66.0%

Source: Congressional Research Service based on analysis of data from the U.S. Census Bureau Current Population Survey (CPS) Annual Social and Economic Supplement (ASEC). See corresponding Figure 4 in the text.

Notes: Disconnected youth are youth who were not working or in school at the time of the survey and were reported as having not worked during the previous year for reasons other than going to school.

Table B-4. Poverty Status of Disconnected and Connected Youth Ages 16-24, by Age Group, 2011 Poverty Status Based on Family Income in 2010 (Numbers in 1,000s)

	Total	Number poor	Poverty Rate (Percent Poor)
Total	38,374	8,111	21.1%
16 - 18	13,096	2,452	18.7%
19 - 21	12,607	2,916	23.1%
22 - 24	12,671	2,743	21.6%
Disconnected	2,641	1,285	48.6%
16 - 18	434	177	40.7%
19 - 21	1,053	501	47.6%
22 - 24	1,155	607	52.5%
Connected	35,733	6,826	19.1%
16 - 18	12,662	2,275	18.0%
19 - 21	11,555	2,415	20.9%
22 - 24	11,517	2,137	18.6%

Source: Congressional Research Service based on analysis of data from the U.S. Census Bureau Current Population Survey (CPS) Annual Social and Economic Supplement (ASEC). See corresponding Figure 5 in the text.

Notes: Disconnected youth are youth who were not working or in school at the time of the survey and were reported as having not worked during the previous year for reasons other than going to school.

Table B-5. Poverty Status of Disconnected and Connected Youth Ages 16-24, by Race and Ethnicity, 2011 Poverty Status Based on Family Income in 2010 (Numbers in 1,000s)

	Total	Number poor	Poverty Rate (Percent Poor)
Total	38,374	8,111	21.1%
White, non-Hispanic	22,638	3,670	16.2%
Black, non-Hispanic	5,438	1,758	32.3%
Hispanic	7,573	2,092	27.6%
Other, non-Hispanic	2,726	592	21.7%
Disconnected	2,641	1,285	48.6%
White, non-Hispanic	1,279	563	44.1%
Black, non-Hispanic	567	328	57.9%
Hispanic	621	327	52.6%
Other, non-Hispanic	174	66	38.1%
Connected	35,733	6,826	19.1%
White, non-Hispanic	21,359	3,106	14.5%
Black, non-Hispanic	4,870	1,429	29.3%
Hispanic	6,953	1,765	25.4%
Other, non-Hispanic	2,551	526	20.6%

Source: Congressional Research Service based on analysis of data from the U.S. Census Bureau Current Population Survey (CPS) Annual Social and Economic Supplement (ASEC).

Notes: Disconnected youth are youth who were not working or in school at the time of the survey and were reported as having not worked during the previous year for reasons other than going to school.

Table B-6. Poverty Status of Disconnected and Connected Youth Ages 19-24, by Level of Educational Attainment, 2011 Poverty Status Based on Family Income in 2010 (Numbers in 1,000s)

	Total	Number poor	Poverty Rate (Percent Poor)
Total	25,279	5,660	22.4%
Lacks HS Diploma	3,001	1,277	42.5%
HS diploma or GED	7,615	1,903	25.0%
Some schooling beyond HS	14,662	2,479	16.9%
Disconnected	2,207	1,108	50.2%
Lacks HS Diploma	669	404	60.4%
HS diploma or GED	1,102	546	49.5%
Some schooling beyond HS	436	158	36.3%
Connected	23,071	4,552	19.7%
Lacks HS Diploma	2,332	873	37.4%
HS diploma or GED	6,513	1,358	20.8%
Some schooling beyond HS	14,226	2,321	16.3%

Source: Congressional Research Service based on analysis of data from the U.S. Census Bureau Current Population Survey (CPS) Annual Social and Economic Supplement (ASEC). See corresponding Figure 6 in the text.

Notes: Disconnected youth are youth who were not working or in school at the time of the survey and were reported as having not worked during the previous year for reasons other than going to school.

Table B-7. Disconnected and Connected Youth Ages 16 to 24 without Health Insurance Coverage, by Age Group, 2011 Uninsured were without Health Insurance During All of 2011 (Numbers in 1,000s)

	Total	Number without health insurance	Percent uninsured
Total	38,374	9,182	23.9%
16 - 18	13,096	1,749	13.4%
19 - 21	12,607	3,385	26.9%
22 - 24	12,671	4,048	31.9%
Disconnected	2,641	1,012	38.3%
16 - 18	434	82	18.9%
19 - 21	1,053	410	38.9%
22 - 24	1,155	519	45.0%
Connected	35,733	8,170	22.9%
16 - 18	12,662	1,666	13.2%
19 - 21	11,555	2,975	25.7%
22 - 24	11,517	3,529	30.6%

Source: Congressional Research Service based on analysis of data from the U.S. Census Bureau Current Population Survey (CPS) Annual Social and Economic Supplement (ASEC). See corresponding Figure 7 in the text.

Notes: Disconnected youth are youth who were not working or in school at the time of the survey and were reported as having not worked during the previous year for reasons other than going to school.

Table B-8. Living Arrangements of Disconnected and Connected Youth Ages 16-24, by Age Group, 2011 (Numbers in 1,000s)

		Age Group		
	Total	16 - 18	19 - 21	22 - 24
All Youth	38,374	13,096	12,607	12,671
Lives with one or both parents	26,203	12,093	8,674	5,435
Lives with both parents	17,412	8,026	5,758	3,628
Lives with only one parent	8,791	4,067	2,916	1,807
Lives apart from parents	12,172	1,002	3,933	7,236
Percent				
Total	100.0%	100.0%	100.0%	100.0%
Lives with one or both parents	68.3%	92.3%	68.8%	42.9%
Lives with both parents	45.4%	61.3%	45.7%	28.6%
Lives with only one parent	22.9%	31.1%	23.1%	14.3%
Lives apart from parents	31.7%	7.7%	31.2%	57.1%
Disconnected Youth	2,641	434	1,053	1,155
Lives with one or both parents	1,543	351	626	565
Lives with both parents	776	186	288	301
Lives with only one parent	768	165	338	264
Lives apart from parents	1,098	83	426	589
Percent				

Table B-8. (Continued)

		Age Group		
	Total	16 - 18	19 - 21	22 - 24
Total	100.0%	100.0%	100.0%	100.0%
Lives with one or both parents	58.4%	80.9%	59.5%	49.0%
Lives with both parents	29.4%	42.9%	27.4%	26.1%
Lives with only one parent	29.1%	38.1%	32.1%	22.9%
Lives apart from parents	41.6%	19.1%	40.5%	51.0%
Connected Youth	35,733	12,662	11,555	11,517
Lives with one or both parents	24,659	11,742	8,048	4,870
Lives with both parents	16,636	7,840	5,469	3,327
Lives with only one parent	8,024	3,902	2,579	1,543
Lives apart from parents	11,073	920	3,507	6,647
Percent				
Total	100.0%	100.0%	100.0%	100.0%
Lives with one or both parents	69.0%	92.7%	69.7%	42.3%
Lives with both parents	46.6%	61.9%	47.3%	28.9%
Lives with only one parent	22.5%	30.8%	22.3%	13.4%
Lives apart from parents	31.0%	7.3%	30.3%	57.7%

Source: Congressional Research Service based on analysis of data from the U.S. Census Bureau Current Population Survey (CPS) Annual Social and Economic Supplement (ASEC). See corresponding Figure 8 in the text.

Notes: Disconnected youth are youth who were not working or in school at the time of the survey and were reported as having not worked during the previous year for reasons other than going to school.

Table B-9. Living Arrangements of Disconnected and Connected Youth Ages 16-24, by Race and Ethnicity, 2011 (Numbers in 1,000s)

		Race and Ethnicity			
	Total	White, non-Hispanic	Black, non-Hispanic	Hispanic	Other, non-Hispanic
All Youth	38,374	22,638	5,438	7,573	2,726
Lives with one or both parents	26,203	15,402	3,604	5,309	1,889
Lives with both parents	17,412	11,431	1,324	3,291	1,365
Lives with only one parent	8,791	3,970	2,279	2,018	524
Lives apart from parents	12,172	7,236	1,834	2,264	837
Percent					
Total	100.0%	100.0%	100.0%	100.0%	100.0%
Lives with one or both parents	68.3%	68.0%	66.3%	70.1%	69.3%
Lives with both parents	45.4%	50.5%	24.4%	43.5%	50.1%

| | | Race and Ethnicity | | | |
	Total	White, non-Hispanic	Black, non-Hispanic	Hispanic	Other, non-Hispanic
Lives with only one parent	22.9%	17.5%	41.9%	26.6%	19.2%
Lives apart from parents	31.7%	32.0%	33.7%	29.9%	30.7%
Disconnected Youth	2,641	1,279	567	621	174
Lives with one or both parents	1,543	746	303	382	111
Lives with both parents	776	446	69	198	62
Lives with only one parent	768	300	234	184	49
Lives apart from parents	1,098	532	264	239	63
Percent					
Total	100.0%	100.0%	100.0%	100.0%	100.0%
Lives with one or both parents	58.4%	58.4%	53.5%	61.6%	63.9%
Lives with both parents	29.4%	34.9%	12.2%	31.9%	35.7%
Lives with only one parent	29.1%	23.5%	41.3%	29.6%	28.2%
Lives apart from parents	41.6%	41.6%	46.5%	38.4%	36.1%
Connected Youth	35,733	21,359	4,870	6,953	2,551
Lives with one or both parents	24,659	14,655	3,300	4,927	1,777
Lives with both parents	16,636	10,985	1,255	3,093	1,303
Lives with only one parent	8,024	3,670	2,045	1,834	475
Lives apart from parents	11,073	6,704	1,570	2,026	774
Percent					
Total	100.0%	100.0%	100.0%	100.0%	100.0%
Lives with one or both parents	69.0%	68.6%	67.8%	70.9%	69.7%
Lives with both parents	46.6%	51.4%	25.8%	44.5%	51.1%
Lives with only one parent	22.5%	17.2%	42.0%	26.4%	18.6%
Lives apart from parents	31.0%	31.4%	32.2%	29.1%	30.3%

Source: Congressional Research Service based on analysis of data from the U.S. Census Bureau Current Population Survey (CPS) Annual Social and Economic Supplement (ASEC).

Notes: Disconnected youth are youth who were not working or in school at the time of the survey and were reported as having not worked during the previous year for reasons other than going to school.

Table B-10. Poverty Status of Disconnected and Connected Youth Ages 16-24, by Living Arrangement, 2011
(Poverty Status Based on Family Income in 2010)

	Total	Lives withboth parents	Lives with only one parent	Lives apart from parents
Total	38,374	17,412	8,791	12,172
Poor	8,111	1,163	2,334	4,615
Poverty rate	21.1%	6.7%	26.5%	37.9%
Disconnected				
Total	2,641	776	768	1,098
Poor	1,285	135	364	786
Poverty rate	48.6%	17.4%	47.4%	71.6%
Connected				
Total	35,733	16,636	8,024	11,073
Poor	6,826	1,028	1,969	3,829
Poverty rate	19.1%	6.2%	24.5%	34.6%

Source: Congressional Research Service based on analysis of data from the U.S. 1988 through 2011 Current Population Survey (CPS) Annual Social and Economic Supplement (ASEC). See corresponding Figure 9 in the text.

Notes: Disconnected youth are youth who were not working or in school at the time of the survey and were reported as having not worked during the previous year for reasons other than going to school.

Table B-11. Educational Attainment of Disconnected and Connected Youths' Parents for Youth Ages 16-24 Living with One or Both Parents, 2011 (Numbers in 1,000s)

	Total		Disconnected		Connected	
	Number	Percent	Number	Percent	Number	Percent
Youth living with one parent only	8,462	100.0%	748	100.0%	7,714	100.0%
Parent lacks a HS education	1,388	16.4%	192	25.6%	1,197	15.5%
Parent has HS diploma or GED	2,885	34.1%	291	38.8%	2,595	33.6%
Parent has some schooling beyond HS	4,189	49.5%	266	35.6%	3,923	50.9%
Youth living with both parents	17,740	100.0%	795	100.0%	16,945	100.0%
One or both parents lack a HS education	3,046	17.2%	252	31.7%	2,795	16.5%

	Total		Disconnected		Connected	
	Number	Percent	Number	Percent	Number	Percent
One or both parents has, and neither is lacking, a HS diploma or GED	6,774	38.2%	339	42.7%	6,435	38.0%
Both parents have some schooling beyond HS	7,920	44.6%	204	25.7%	7,716	45.5%

Source: Congressional Research Service based on analysis of data from the U.S. Census Bureau Current Population Survey (CPS) Annual Social and Economic Supplement (ASEC). See corresponding Figure 10 in the text.

Notes: Disconnected youth are youth who were not working or in school at the time of the survey and were reported as having not worked during the previous year for reasons other than going to school.

Table B-12. Employment Status of Disconnected and Connected Youths' Parents, for Youth Ages 16 to 24 Living with One or Both Parents, 2011 (Numbers in 1,000s)

	Total		Disconnected		Connected	
	Number	Percent	Number	Percent	Number	Percent
Youth living with one						
parent only	8,344	100.0%	630	100.0%	7,714	100.0%
Parent employed	5,888	70.6%	361	57.3%	5,527	71.6%
Parent not employed	2,456	29.4%	269	42.7%	2,187	28.4%
Youth living with both parents	17,740	100.0%	795	100.0%	16,945	100.0%
One or both parents employed	16,619	93.7%	673	84.6%	15,946	94.1%
Only father employed	4,276	24.1%	227	28.6%	4,049	23.9%
Only mother employed	1,760	9.9%	118	14.9%	1,642	9.7%
Both parents employed	10,584	59.7%	328	41.2%	10,256	60.5%
Neither parent employed	1,121	6.3%	122	15.4%	999	5.9%

Source: Congressional Research Service based on analysis of data from the U.S. Census Bureau Current Population Survey (CPS) Annual Social and Economic Supplement (ASEC). See corresponding Figure 11 in the text.

Notes: Disconnected youth are youth who were not working or in school at the time of the survey and were reported as having not worked during the previous year for reasons other than going to school.

Appendix C. Background Tables for Congressional Research Service Analysis of Disconnected Youth, 1988-2011

Table C-1.Total and Disconnected Youth Ages 16-24, by Gender, 1988-2011 (Numbers in 1,000s)

| | | | | | Males | | | Females | |
| | | Disconnected | | | Disconnected | | | Disconnected | |
Year	Total	Number	Rate	Total	Number	Rate	Total	Number	Rate
1988	33,460	1,608	4.8%	16,614	605	3.6%	16,847	1,003	6.0%
1989	32,646	1,508	4.6%	16,147	497	3.1%	16,499	1,011	6.1%
1990	31,942	1,316	4.1%	15,844	388	2.4%	16,098	928	5.8%
1991	31,522	1,453	4.6%	15,672	502	3.2%	15,850	951	6.0%
1992	31,037	1,480	4.8%	15,458	517	3.3%	15,578	963	6.2%
1993	30,967	1,575	5.1%	15,439	535	3.5%	15,527	1,041	6.7%
1994	32,654	2,169	6.6%	16,379	831	5.1%	16,276	1,338	8.2%
1995	32,515	1,675	5.2%	16,304	616	3.8%	16,211	1,059	6.5%
1996	32,399	1,662	5.1%	16,287	627	3.9%	16,112	1,034	6.4%
1997	32,800	1,476	4.5%	16,562	629	3.8%	16,238	847	5.2%
1998	33,137	1,413	4.3%	16,739	603	3.6%	16,397	810	4.9%
1999	34,023	1,321	3.9%	17,118	579	3.4%	16,905	742	4.4%
2000	34,614	1,350	3.9%	17,499	559	3.2%	17,116	791	4.6%
2001	34,758	1,448	4.2%	17,506	593	3.4%	17,252	856	5.0%
2002	35,434	1,646	4.6%	17,860	695	3.9%	17,574	951	5.4%
2003	35,958	1,669	4.6%	18,140	744	4.1%	17,818	925	5.2%
2004	36,545	1,721	4.7%	18,497	781	4.2%	18,048	940	5.2%
2005	36,749	1,914	5.2%	18,586	887	4.8%	18,163	1,027	5.7%
2006	36,978	1,842	5.0%	18,726	809	4.3%	18,251	1,032	5.7%
2007	37,482	1,829	4.9%	19,018	753	4.0%	18,465	1,075	5.8%
2008	37,580	1,915	5.1%	19,032	722	3.8%	18,548	1,193	6.4%
2009	37,740	2,207	5.8%	19,103	1,025	5.4%	18,636	1,183	6.3%
2010	36,168	2,837	7.4%	19,328	1,430	7.4%	18,389	1,407	7.5%
2011	38,374	2,641	6.9%	19,585	1,254	6.4%	18,790	1,387	7.4%

Source: Congressional Research Service based on analysis of data from the U.S. Census Bureau Current Population Survey (CPS) Annual Social and Economic Supplement (ASEC). See corresponding Figure 12 in the text.

Notes: Disconnected youth are youth who were not working or in school at the time of the survey and were reported as having not worked during the previous year for reasons other than going to school.

Table C-2. Disconnected Males Ages 16-24, by Age Group, 1988-2011
(Numbers in 1,000s)

	Age 16 - 18			Age 19 - 21			Age 22 - 24		
		Total			Disconnected			Disconnected	
Year	Total	Number	Rate	Total	Number	Rate	Total	Number	Rate
1988	5,630	77	1.4%	5,208	224	4.3%	5,775	305	5.3%
1989	5,411	103	1.9%	5,066	178	3.5%	5,669	216	3.8%
1990	5,183	86	1.7%	5,356	162	3.0%	5,305	140	2.6%
1991	5,075	111	2.2%	5,255	224	4.3%	5,341	166	3.1%
1992	4,985	111	2.2%	5,112	201	3.9%	5,361	205	3.8%
1993	5,064	102	2.0%	4,880	192	3.9%	5,496	240	4.4%
1994	5,388	219	4.1%	5,139	280	5.4%	5,851	332	5.7%
1995	5,493	153	2.8%	5,214	226	4.3%	5,598	237	4.2%
1996	5,719	165	2.9%	5,184	253	4.9%	5,384	209	3.9%
1997	5,883	168	2.9%	5,422	225	4.1%	5,256	236	4.5%
1998	6,031	172	2.9%	5,525	246	4.5%	5,183	184	3.6%
1999	6,232	174	2.8%	5,659	238	4.2%	5,227	167	3.2%
2000	6,209	107	1.7%	5,988	288	4.8%	5,302	164	3.1%
2001	6,207	114	1.8%	5,809	258	4.4%	5,491	220	4.0%
2002	6,147	163	2.7%	6,160	319	5.2%	5,553	214	3.8%
2003	6,337	188	3.0%	6,004	303	5.0%	5,799	253	4.4%
2004	6,441	140	2.2%	6,076	328	5.4%	5,979	313	5.2%
2005	6,492	208	3.2%	5,941	350	5.9%	6,153	329	5.3%
2006	6,617	163	2.5%	6,046	342	5.7%	6,063	304	5.0%
2007	6,742	147	2.2%	6,128	332	5.4%	6,147	274	4.5%
2008	6,816	142	2.1%	5,926	294	5.0%	6,290	286	4.5%
2009	6,744	208	3.1%	6,135	423	6.9%	6,224	394	6.3%
2010	6,690	267	4.0%	6,399	649	10.1%	6,239	514	8.2%
2011	6,725	209	3.1%	6,389	523	8.2%	6,471	523	8.1%

Source: Congressional Research Service based on analysis of data from the U.S. Census Bureau Current Population Survey (CPS) Annual Social and Economic Supplement (ASEC). See corresponding Figure 13 in the text.

Notes: Disconnected youth are youth who were not working or in school at the time of the survey and were reported as having not worked during the previous year for reasons other than going to school.

**Table C-3. Disconnected Females Ages 16-24, by Age Group, 1988-2011
(Numbers in 1,000s)**

	Age 16 - 18			Age 19 - 21			Age 22 - 24		
		Total			Disconnected			Disconnected	
Year	Total	Number	Rate	Total	Number	Rate	Total	Number	Rate
1988	5,426	119	2.2%	5,601	389	7.0%	5,820	495	8.5%
1989	5,319	163	3.1%	5,448	396	7.3%	5,733	453	7.9%
1990	5,005	142	2.8%	5,459	333	6.1%	5,634	454	8.1%
1991	4,874	142	2.9%	5,487	369	6.7%	5,489	440	8.0%
1992	4,810	171	3.5%	5,242	394	7.5%	5,527	399	7.2%
1993	4,864	156	3.2%	5,042	422	8.4%	5,621	462	8.2%
1994	5,207	257	4.9%	5,283	555	10.5%	5,786	525	9.1%
1995	5,328	200	3.7%	5,080	370	7.3%	5,802	490	8.4%
1996	5,455	201	3.7%	5,308	434	8.2%	5,349	400	7.5%
1997	5,604	169	3.0%	5,533	352	6.4%	5,100	326	6.4%
1998	5,715	138	2.4%	5,481	345	6.3%	5,201	328	6.3%
1999	5,806	141	2.4%	5,762	354	6.1%	5,337	247	4.6%
2000	5,890	162	2.8%	5,772	342	5.9%	5,454	287	5.3%
2001	5,821	176	3.0%	5,786	343	5.9%	5,645	336	6.0%
2002	5,907	159	2.7%	5,952	448	7.5%	5,716	344	6.0%
2003	6,147	145	2.4%	5,738	354	6.2%	5,933	426	7.2%
2004	6,307	164	2.6%	5,681	322	5.7%	6,061	454	7.5%
2005	6,224	157	2.5%	5,784	418	7.2%	6,155	452	7.3%
2006	6,320	155	2.5%	5,711	419	7.3%	6,220	458	7.4%
2007	6,440	163	2.5%	5,935	424	7.1%	6,090	488	8.0%
2008	6,615	209	3.2%	5,794	448	7.7%	6,139	536	8.7%
2009	6,480	185	2.9%	5,846	463	7.9%	6,310	535	8.5%
2010	6,442	208	3.2%	6,123	589	9.6%	6,274	610	9.7%
2011	6,371	226	3.5%	6,219	530	8.5%	6,200	632	10.2%

Source: Congressional Research Service based on analysis of data from the U.S.
Census Bureau Current Population Survey (CPS) Annual Social and Economic
Supplement (ASEC). See corresponding Figure 14 in the text.

Notes: Disconnected youth are youth who were not working or in school at the time of
the survey and were reported as having not worked during the previous year for
reasons other than going to school.

Table C-4. Disconnected Males Ages 16-24, by Race and Ethnicity, 1988-2011 (Numbers in 1,000s)

| Year | White, Non-Hispanic | | | Black, Non-Hispanic | | | | Hispanic | |
| | Total | Disconnected | | Total | Disconnected | | Total | Disconnected | |
		Number	Rate		Number	Rate		Number	Rate
1988	12,097	319	2.6%	2,238	185	8.3%	1,690	89	5.3%
1989	11,679	266	2.3%	2,190	159	7.3%	1,695	57	3.4%
1990	11,344	192	1.7%	2,190	127	5.8%	1,752	56	3.2%
1991	11,085	204	1.8%	2,155	198	9.2%	1,801	85	4.7%
1992	10,860	224	2.1%	2,155	198	9.2%	1,810	76	4.2%
1993	10,883	232	2.1%	2,176	212	9.8%	1,781	72	4.0%
1994	11,243	446	4.0%	2,248	206	9.2%	2,228	156	7.0%
1995	11,158	243	2.2%	2,249	219	9.8%	2,297	137	5.9%
1996	10,889	254	2.3%	2,236	211	9.4%	2,339	135	5.8%
1997	10,948	243	2.2%	2,295	230	10.0%	2,568	124	4.8%
1998	11,063	269	2.4%	2,293	174	7.6%	2,617	136	5.2%
1999	11,286	270	2.4%	2,352	171	7.3%	2,609	118	4.5%
2000	11,409	208	1.8%	2,422	215	8.9%	2,659	112	4.2%
2001	11,017	214	1.9%	2,316	235	10.2%	3,162	116	3.7%
2002	11,217	318	2.8%	2,374	231	9.7%	3,202	110	3.4%
2003	11,346	296	2.6%	2,351	293	12.4%	3,253	114	3.5%
2004	11,542	343	3.0%	2,395	252	10.5%	3,338	153	4.6%
2005	11,569	376	3.2%	2,453	292	11.9%	3,346	176	5.3%
2006	11,608	352	3.0%	2,517	258	10.2%	3,350	153	4.6%
2007	11,685	356	3.0%	2,584	232	9.0%	3,449	112	3.2%
2008	11,744	358	3.0%	2,587	176	6.8%	3,435	137	4.0%
2009	11,725	509	4.3%	2,623	280	10.7%	3,467	175	5.0%
2010	11,643	678	5.8%	2,662	366	13.7%	3,692	292	7.9%
2011	11,480	617	5.4%	2,645	274	10.3%	4,086	286	7.0%

Source: Congressional Research Service based on analysis of data from the U.S. Census Bureau Current Population Survey (CPS) Annual Social and Economic Supplement (ASEC). See corresponding Figure 15 in the text.

Notes: Disconnected youth are youth who were not working or in school at the time of the survey and were reported as having not worked during the previous year for reasons other than going to school. Non-Hispanic youth of races other than white and black are not depicted due to small sample sizes. Racial categories for 2003 and after are not directly comparable to earlier years. Beginning in 2003, respondents were able to report more than one race on the CPS, whereas before they could only report a single race. The data for 2003 and after reflect the race of respondents who reported only one race.

Table C-5. Disconnected Females Ages 16-24, by Race and Ethnicity, 1988-2011 (Numbers in 1,000s)

| Year | White, Non-Hispanic | | | Black, Non-Hispanic | | | | Hispanic | |
| | Total | Disconnected | | Total | Disconnected | | Total | Disconnected | |
		Number	Rate		Number	Rate		Number	Rate
1988	12,241	407	3.3%	2,449	367	15.0%	1,609	186	11.6%
1989	11,916	444	3.7%	2,417	346	14.3%	1,586	190	12.0%
1990	11,503	427	3.7%	2,402	297	12.4%	1,628	174	10.7%
1991	11,211	416	3.7%	2,357	312	13.2%	1,679	189	11.3%
1992	10,951	409	3.7%	2,347	317	13.5%	1,729	198	11.5%
1993	10,833	393	3.6%	2,357	355	15.1%	1,748	253	14.5%
1994	11,057	614	5.6%	2,490	354	14.2%	2,068	326	15.7%
1995	11,045	419	3.8%	2,501	326	13.0%	2,046	272	13.3%
1996	10,609	454	4.3%	2,477	273	11.0%	2,201	272	12.3%
1997	10,781	356	3.3%	2,496	221	8.9%	2,139	229	10.7%
1998	10,834	348	3.2%	2,538	195	7.7%	2,240	224	10.0%
1999	10,979	320	2.9%	2,605	164	6.3%	2,421	223	9.2%
2000	11,149	297	2.7%	2,636	178	6.7%	2,431	251	10.3%
2001	10,863	349	3.2%	2,570	198	7.7%	2,796	247	8.9%
2002	11,048	347	3.1%	2,626	250	9.5%	2,858	297	10.4%
2003	11,165	388	3.5%	2,583	209	8.1%	2,853	261	9.1%
2004	11,250	396	3.5%	2,630	223	8.5%	2,951	246	8.4%
2005	11,312	460	4.1%	2,632	213	8.1%	2,990	274	9.2%
2006	11,314	440	3.9%	2,675	258	9.7%	3,034	260	8.6%
2007	11,317	479	4.2%	2,718	258	9.5%	3,136	271	8.6%
2008	11,332	481	4.2%	2,752	307	11.2%	3,188	301	9.4%
2009	11,332	533	4.7%	2,794	271	9.7%	3,253	304	9.4%
2010	11,299	611	5.4%	2,806	343	12.2%	3,418	361	10.6%
2011	11,157	662	5.9%	2,793	294	10.5%	3,487	335	9.6%

Source: Congressional Research Service based on analysis of data from the U.S. Census Bureau Current Population Survey (CPS) Annual Social and Economic Supplement (ASEC). See corresponding Figure 16 in the text.

Notes: Disconnected youth are youth who were not working or in school at the time of the survey and were reported as having not worked during the previous year for reasons other than going to school. Non-Hispanic youth of races other than white and black are not depicted due to small sample sizes. Racial categories for 2003 and after are not directly comparable to earlier years. Beginning in 2003, respondents were able to report more than one race on the CPS, whereas before they could only report a single race. The data for 2003 and after reflect the race of respondents who reported only one race.

Table C-6. Disconnected Female Youth Ages 16-24, by Parental Status, Race, and Ethnicity, 1988- 2008
(Numbers in 1,000s)

	Total	Discon-nected	Discon-nection rate	Disconnected No child(ren)	Disconnected Has child(ren)	Share of total whoare disconnected No child(ren)	Share of total whoare disconnected Has child(ren)
Total							
1988	16,847	1,003	6.0%	389	613	2.3%	3.6%
1989	16,499	1,011	6.1%	386	625	2.3%	3.8%
1990	16,098	928	5.8%	406	523	2.5%	3.2%
1991	15,850	951	6.0%	373	578	2.4%	3.6%
1992	15,578	963	6.2%	389	574	2.5%	3.7%
1993	15,527	1,041	6.7%	392	648	2.5%	4.2%
1994	16,276	1,338	8.2%	682	656	4.2%	4.0%
1995	16,211	1,059	6.5%	534	525	3.3%	3.2%
1996	16,112	1,034	6.4%	519	515	3.2%	3.2%
1997	16,238	847	5.2%	447	400	2.8%	2.5%
1998	16,397	810	4.9%	463	347	2.8%	2.1%
1999	16,905	742	4.4%	473	269	2.8%	1.6%
2000	17,116	791	4.6%	525	266	3.1%	1.6%
2001	17,252	856	5.0%	564	292	3.3%	1.7%
2002	17,574	951	5.4%	615	335	3.5%	1.9%
2003	17,818	925	5.2%	585	339	3.3%	1.9%
2004	18,048	940	5.2%	607	333	3.4%	1.8%
2005	18,163	1,027	5.7%	639	388	3.5%	2.1%
2006	18,251	1,032	5.7%	647	385	3.5%	2.1%
2007	18,465	1,075	5.8%	741	334	4.0%	1.8%
2008	18,548	1,194	6.4%	796	398	4.3%	2.1%
2009	18,636	1,183	6.3%	731	451	3.9%	2.4%
2010	18,839	1,407	7.5%	895	512	4.8%	2.7%
2011	18,790	1,387	7.4%	864	523	4.6%	2.8%
White, Non-Hispanic							
1988	12,241	407	3.3%	197	210	1.6%	1.7%
1989	11,916	444	3.7%	207	237	1.7%	2.0%
1990	11,503	427	3.7%	213	213	1.9%	1.9%
1991	11,211	416	3.7%	190	226	1.7%	2.0%
1992	10,951	409	3.7%	162	247	1.5%	2.3%
1993	10,833	393	3.6%	163	229	1.5%	2.1%
1994	11,057	614	5.6%	343	271	3.1%	2.5%
1995	11,045	419	3.8%	238	181	2.2%	1.6%
1996	10,609	454	4.3%	266	188	2.5%	1.8%
1997	10,781	356	3.3%	229	127	2.1%	1.2%
1998	10,834	348	3.2%	212	136	2.0%	1.3%
1999	10,979	320	2.9%	213	106	1.9%	1.0%
2000	11,149	297	2.7%	205	93	1.8%	0.8%

Table C-6. (Continued)

	Total	Discon-nected	Discon-nection rate	Disconnected No child(ren)	Has child(ren)	Share of total whoare disconnected No child(ren)	Has child(ren)
2001	10,863	349	3.2%	255	94	2.3%	0.9%
2002	11,048	347	3.1%	249	98	2.3%	0.9%
2003	11,165	388	3.5%	261	128	2.3%	1.1%
2004	11,250	396	3.5%	287	109	2.5%	1.0%
2005	11,312	460	4.1%	300	159	2.7%	1.4%
2006	11,314	440	3.9%	270	170	2.4%	1.5%
2007	11,317	479	4.2%	344	135	3.0%	1.2%
2008	11,332	481	4.2%	352	129	3.1%	1.1%
2009	11,322	533	4.7%	350	184	3.1%	1.6%
2010	11,299	611	5.4%	413	198	3.7%	1.8%
2011	11,157	662	5.9%	446	216	4.0%	1.9%
Black, Non-Hispanic							
1988	2,449	367	15.0%	96	271	3.9%	11.0%
1989	2,417	346	14.3%	75	271	3.1%	11.2%
1990	2,402	297	12.4%	88	209	3.7%	8.7%
1991	2,357	312	13.2%	76	236	3.2%	10.0%
1992	2,347	317	13.5%	94	223	4.0%	9.5%
1993	2,357	355	15.1%	88	267	3.8%	11.3%
1994	2,490	354	14.2%	127	227	5.1%	9.1%
1995	2,501	326	13.0%	123	204	4.9%	8.1%
1996	2,477	273	11.0%	99	174	4.0%	7.0%
1997	2,496	221	8.9%	85	136	3.4%	5.4%
1998	2,538	195	7.7%	89	107	3.5%	4.2%
1999	2,605	164	6.3%	88	76	3.4%	2.9%
2000	2,636	178	6.7%	100	78	3.8%	3.0%
2001	2,570	198	7.7%	97	101	3.8%	3.9%
2002	2,626	250	9.5%	145	105	5.5%	4.0%
2003	2,583	209	8.1%	110	99	4.3%	3.8%
2004	2,630	223	8.5%	113	110	4.3%	4.2%
2005	2,632	213	8.1%	114	99	4.3%	3.7%
2006	2,675	258	9.7%	155	103	5.8%	3.9%
2007	2,718	258	9.5%	156	103	5.7%	3.8%
2008	2,752	307	11.2%	176	131	6.4%	4.8%
2009	2,794	271	9.7%	152	119	5.4%	4.3%
2010	2,806	343	12.2%	213	130	7.6%	4.6%
2011	2,793	294	10.5%	181	113	6.5%	4.0%
Hispanic							
1988	1,609	186	11.6%	71	115	4.4%	7.1%
1989	1,586	190	12.0%	87	103	5.5%	6.5%
1990	1,628	174	10.7%	92	82	5.7%	5.0%
1991	1,679	189	11.3%	89	100	5.3%	6.0%

	Total	Discon-nected	Discon-nection rate	Disconnected		Share of total whoare disconnected	
				No child(ren)	Has child(ren)	No child(ren)	Has child(ren)
1992	1,729	198	11.5%	107	91	6.2%	5.2%
1993	1,748	253	14.5%	122	131	7.0%	7.5%
1994	2,068	326	15.7%	185	140	9.0%	6.8%
1995	2,046	272	13.3%	151	122	7.4%	6.0%
1996	2,201	272	12.3%	132	140	6.0%	6.4%
1997	2,139	229	10.7%	103	126	4.8%	5.9%
1998	2,240	224	10.0%	122	102	5.5%	4.6%
1999	2,421	223	9.2%	147	76	6.1%	3.1%
2000	2,431	251	10.3%	165	87	6.8%	3.6%
2001	2,796	247	8.9%	165	82	5.9%	2.9%
2002	2,858	297	10.4%	179	118	6.3%	4.1%
2003	2,853	261	9.1%	161	100	5.7%	3.5%
2004	2,951	246	8.4%	159	87	5.4%	3.0%
2005	2,990	274	9.2%	170	104	5.7%	3.5%
2006	3,034	260	8.6%	163	97	5.4%	3.2%
2007	3,136	271	8.6%	191	79	6.1%	2.5%
2008	3,188	302	9.5%	185	117	5.8%	3.7%
2009	3,253	304	9.4%	173	131	5.3%	4.0%
2010	3,418	361	10.6%	194	167	5.7%	4.9%
2011	3,487	335	9.6%	165	170	4.7%	4.9%

Source: Congressional Research Service based on analysis of data from the U.S. 1988 through 2011 Current Population Survey (CPS) Annual Social and Economic Supplement (ASEC). See corresponding Figure 17, Figure 18, and Figure 19 in the text.

Notes: Disconnected youth are youth who were not working or in school at the time of the survey and were reported as having not worked during the previous year for reasons other than going to school. Details may not sum to totals due to rounding. Non-Hispanic persons other than whites and blacks are included in the total but are not shown separately, due to small sample sizes.

Table C-7. Single Mothers Ages 16 to 24, by Connected and Disconnected Status, Race and Ethnicity, 1988-2011 (Numbers in 1,000s)

Year	Total female youth	Total	Connect-ed	Discon-nected	Single mothers as a percent of all female youth			Composition of single mothers	
					Total	Connected	Discon-nected	Connect-ed	Discon-nected
Total									
1988	16,847	1,565	1,050	514	9.3%	6.2%	3.1%	67.1%	32.9%
1989	16,499	1,624	1,082	542	9.8%	6.6%	3.3%	66.6%	33.4%
1990	16,098	1,533	1,044	489	9.5%	6.5%	3.0%	68.1%	31.9%

Table C-7. (Continued)

Year	Total female youth	Total	Connect-ed	Discon-nected	Single mothers as a percent of all female youth			Composition of single mothers	
					Total	Connected	Discon-nected	Connect-ed	Discon-nected
1991	15,850	1,601	1,073	529	10.1%	6.8%	3.3%	67.0%	33.0%
1992	15,578	1,643	1,119	524	10.5%	7.2%	3.4%	68.1%	31.9%
1993	15,527	1,789	1,202	587	11.5%	7.7%	3.8%	67.2%	32.8%
1994	16,276	1,882	1,270	612	11.6%	7.8%	3.8%	67.5%	32.5%
1995	16,211	1,878	1,396	481	11.6%	8.6%	3.0%	74.4%	25.6%
1996	16,112	1,867	1,388	480	11.6%	8.6%	3.0%	74.3%	25.7%
1997	16,238	1,936	1,567	369	11.9%	9.6%	2.3%	80.9%	19.1%
1998	16,397	1,843	1,520	322	11.2%	9.3%	2.0%	82.5%	17.5%
1999	16,905	1,830	1,576	254	10.8%	9.3%	1.5%	86.1%	13.9%
2000	17,116	1,932	1,688	244	11.3%	9.9%	1.4%	87.4%	12.6%
2001	17,252	1,772	1,507	266	10.3%	8.7%	1.5%	85.0%	15.0%
2002	17,574	1,798	1,490	308	10.2%	8.5%	1.8%	82.9%	17.1%
2003	17,818	1,802	1,488	314	10.1%	8.3%	1.8%	82.6%	17.4%
2004	18,048	1,841	1,533	308	10.2%	8.5%	1.7%	83.3%	16.7%
2005	18,163	1,850	1,486	365	10.2%	8.2%	2.0%	80.3%	19.7%
2006	18,251	1,793	1,437	355	9.8%	7.9%	1.9%	80.2%	19.8%
2007	18,465	1,644	1,333	311	8.9%	7.2%	1.7%	81.1%	18.9%
2008	18,548	1,589	1,214	376	8.6%	6.5%	2.0%	76.4%	23.6%
2009	18,636	1,894	1,476	418	10.2%	7.9%	2.2%	77.9%	22.1%
2010	18,839	1,945	1,473	473	10.3%	7.8%	2.5%	75.7%	24.3%
2011	18,790	1,963	1,488	476	10.4%	7.9%	2.5%	75.8%	24.2%
White, Non-Hispanic									
1988	12,241	640	488	153	5.2%	4.0%	1.2%	76.2%	23.8%
1989	11,916	694	511	184	5.8%	4.3%	1.5%	73.5%	26.5%
1990	11,503	680	495	185	5.9%	4.3%	1.6%	72.8%	27.2%
1991	11,211	736	530	206	6.6%	4.7%	1.8%	72.1%	27.9%
1992	10,951	770	555	215	7.0%	5.1%	2.0%	72.0%	28.0%
1993	10,833	818	615	203	7.5%	5.7%	1.9%	75.2%	24.8%
1994	11,057	900	649	251	8.1%	5.9%	2.3%	72.1%	27.9%
1995	11,045	880	722	158	8.0%	6.5%	1.4%	82.1%	17.9%
1996	10,609	822	643	179	7.7%	6.1%	1.7%	78.2%	21.8%
1997	10,781	905	791	113	8.4%	7.3%	1.1%	87.5%	12.5%
1998	10,834	850	720	130	7.8%	6.6%	1.2%	84.7%	15.3%
1999	10,979	839	736	103	7.6%	6.7%	0.9%	87.7%	12.3%
2000	11,149	840	755	85	7.5%	6.8%	0.8%	89.9%	10.1%
2001	10,863	749	674	75	6.9%	6.2%	0.7%	90.0%	10.0%
2002	11,048	763	682	81	6.9%	6.2%	0.7%	89.4%	10.6%
2003	11,165	783	668	115	7.0%	6.0%	1.0%	85.4%	14.6%
2004	11,250	785	679	106	7.0%	6.0%	0.9%	86.5%	13.5%
2005	11,312	877	734	143	7.8%	6.5%	1.3%	83.7%	16.3%
2006	11,314	838	683	155	7.4%	6.0%	1.4%	81.5%	18.5%

Year	Total female youth	Total	Connect-ed	Discon-nected	Single mothers as a percent of all female youth			Composition of single mothers	
					Total	Connected	Discon-nected	Connected	Discon-nected
2007	11,317	720	598	122	6.4%	5.3%	1.1%	83.1%	16.9%
2008	11,332	615	497	118	5.4%	4.4%	1.0%	80.9%	19.1%
2009	11,322	826	667	159	7.3%	5.9%	1.4%	80.7%	19.3%
2010	11,299	821	640	181	7.3%	5.7%	1.6%	78.0%	22.0%
2011	11,157	886	693	192	7.9%	6.2%	1.7%	78.3%	21.7%
Black, Non-Hispanic									
1988	2,449	680	420	260	27.8%	17.1%	10.6%	61.7%	38.3%
1989	2,417	723	463	261	29.9%	19.1%	10.8%	64.0%	36.0%
1990	2,402	627	421	206	26.1%	17.5%	8.6%	67.1%	32.9%
1991	2,357	649	423	226	27.5%	17.9%	9.6%	65.2%	34.8%
1992	2,347	647	431	216	27.6%	18.4%	9.2%	66.7%	33.3%
1993	2,357	663	412	251	28.1%	17.5%	10.7%	62.1%	37.9%
1994	2,490	689	467	222	27.7%	18.8%	8.9%	67.8%	32.2%
1995	2,501	682	480	202	27.3%	19.2%	8.1%	70.3%	29.7%
1996	2,477	641	469	171	25.9%	18.9%	6.9%	73.2%	26.8%
1997	2,496	644	511	133	25.8%	20.5%	5.3%	79.3%	20.7%
1998	2,538	625	534	91	24.6%	21.0%	3.6%	85.4%	14.6%
1999	2,605	608	535	73	23.4%	20.5%	2.8%	87.9%	12.1%
2000	2,636	698	628	69	26.5%	23.8%	2.6%	90.1%	9.9%
2001	2,570	584	483	101	22.7%	18.8%	3.9%	82.6%	17.4%
2002	2,626	594	491	103	22.6%	18.7%	3.9%	82.7%	17.3%
2003	2,583	556	457	98	21.5%	17.7%	3.8%	82.3%	17.7%
2004	2,630	603	499	104	22.9%	19.0%	3.9%	82.8%	17.2%
2005	2,632	522	425	97	19.8%	16.2%	3.7%	81.5%	18.5%
2006	2,675	504	405	99	18.8%	15.2%	3.7%	80.4%	19.6%
2007	2,718	513	410	103	18.9%	15.1%	3.8%	79.9%	20.1%
2008	2,752	510	379	131	18.5%	13.8%	4.8%	74.3%	25.7%
2009	2,794	512	400	112	18.3%	14.3%	4.0%	78.1%	21.9%
2010	2,806	544	418	126	19.4%	14.9%	4.5%	76.9%	23.1%
2011	2,793	485	378	106	17.4%	13.6%	3.8%	78.1%	21.9%
Hispanic									
1988	1,609	214	128	86	13.3%	7.9%	5.4%	59.7%	40.3%
1989	1,586	166	80	85	10.4%	5.1%	5.4%	48.4%	51.6%
1990	1,628	188	109	80	11.6%	6.7%	4.9%	57.7%	42.3%
1991	1,679	176	93	83	10.5%	5.5%	4.9%	52.9%	47.1%
1992	1,729	190	111	80	11.0%	6.4%	4.6%	58.3%	41.7%
1993	1,748	264	152	112	15.1%	8.7%	6.4%	57.4%	42.6%
1994	2,068	242	120	122	11.7%	5.8%	5.9%	49.7%	50.3%
1995	2,046	271	160	110	13.2%	7.8%	5.4%	59.2%	40.8%
1996	2,201	329	213	116	14.9%	9.7%	5.3%	64.7%	35.3%
1997	2,139	340	225	114	15.9%	10.5%	5.4%	66.3%	33.7%
1998	2,240	335	237	98	15.0%	10.6%	4.4%	70.6%	29.4%
1999	2,421	332	263	69	13.7%	10.9%	2.9%	79.2%	20.8%
2000	2,431	333	252	81	13.7%	10.3%	3.3%	75.6%	24.4%

Table C-7. (Continued)

Year	Total female youth	Total	Connect-ed	Discon-nected	Single mothers as a percent of all female youth			Composition of single mothers	
					Total	Connected	Discon-nected	Connect-ed	Discon-nected
2001	2,796	360	284	76	12.9%	10.2%	2.7%	78.9%	21.1%
2002	2,858	373	263	110	13.1%	9.2%	3.8%	70.6%	29.4%
2003	2,853	384	292	92	13.4%	10.2%	3.2%	76.0%	24.0%
2004	2,951	369	289	80	12.5%	9.8%	2.7%	78.3%	21.7%
2005	2,990	371	271	100	12.4%	9.1%	3.4%	72.9%	27.1%
2006	3,034	358	270	88	11.8%	8.9%	2.9%	75.3%	24.7%
2007	3,136	353	282	71	11.3%	9.0%	2.3%	79.8%	20.2%
2008	3,188	380	271	109	11.9%	8.5%	3.4%	71.4%	28.6%
2009	3,253	465	334	130	14.3%	10.3%	4.0%	72.0%	28.0%
2010	3,418	510	356	154	14.9%	10.4%	4.5%	69.8%	30.2%
2011	3,487	509	351	158	14.6%	10.1%	4.5%	69.0%	31.0%

Source: Congressional Research Service based on analysis of data from the U.S. 1988 through 2011 Current Population Survey (CPS) Annual Social and Economic Supplement (ASEC). See corresponding Figure 20 in the text .

Notes: Disconnected youth are youth who were not working or in school at the time of the survey and were reported as having not worked during the previous year for reasons other than going to school. Details may not sum to totals due to rounding. Non-Hispanic persons other than whites and blacks are included in the total but are not shown separately, due to small sample sizes.

End Notes

[1] Authorization for most of these programs expired at the end of FY2008. For additional information about ESEA, see CRS Report RL33960, *The Elementary and Secondary Education Act, as Amended by the No Child Left Behind Act: A Primer*, by Rebecca R. Skinner.

[2] Authorization of appropriations under WIA expired at the end of FY2003 but has been annually extended through appropriations acts. For additional information about WIA youth programs, see CRS Report R40929, *Vulnerable Youth: Employment and Job Training Programs*, by Adrienne L. Fernandes-Alcantara.

[3] The CPS/ASEC is administered in February through April, though the majority of respondents are surveyed in March.

[4] In 2009, the most recent year for which data are available, 86,927 youth (including those over age 18) were placed in residential juvenile justice facilities. Department of Justice, Office of Justice Programs, Office of Juvenile Justice and Delinquency Prevention, *Census of Juveniles in Residential Placement.* On one day in 2007, the most recent year for which data are available, 747,800 youth ages 18 through 24 were held in state or federal prisons or

local jails. Department of Justice, Bureau of Justice Statistics, *Prison Inmates at Midyear 2009*, Table 17.

[5] For information about existing federal policies and programs targeting vulnerable youth, see CRS Report RL33975, *Vulnerable Youth: Background and Policies*, by Adrienne L. Fernandes-Alcantara. For background on youth unemployment and educational attainment, and factors contributing to youth joblessness, see CRS Report RL32871, *Youth: From Classroom to Workplace?*, by Linda Levine. For information about graduation rates and federal programs to target youth who have dropped out, see CRS Report RL33963, *High School Graduation, Completion, and Dropouts: Federal Policy, Programs, and Issues*, by Jeffrey J. Kuenzi.

[6] U.S. Congress, House Ways and Means Committee, Income Security and Family Support Subcommittee, "Hearing on Disconnected and Disadvantaged Youth," June 19, 2007, available at http://waysandmeans.house.gov/hearings.asp? formmode=detail&hearing=569.

[7] Ibid. See for example, the testimony of Ronald B. Mincy, Professor of Social Policy and Social Work Practice at Columbia University.

[8] To date, there has not been an attempt to quantify the cost of disconnection, though at least two studies discuss the types of costs that might be incurred by unemployed youth and in the U.S. economy. See Andrew Sum et al., *Still Young, Restless, and Jobless: The Growing Employment Malaise Among U.S. Teens and Young Adults*, Northeastern University Center for Labor Market Studies, January 2004, pp. 19-21. See Brett V. Brown and Carol Emig, "Prevalence, Patterns, and Outcomes" in Douglas J. Besharov, *America's Disconnected Youth: Toward a Preventative Strategy* (Washington, D.C.: Child Welfare League of America, 1999), pp. 101-102.

[9] U.S. Government Accountability Office, *Disconnected Youth: Federal Action Could Address Some of the Challenges Faced by Local Programs That Reconnect Youth Education and Employment*, GAO-08-313, February 2008.

[10] The GAO report did not independently evaluate the number of disconnected youth. According to this definition, foster youth emancipating from foster care with weak family support would be considered disconnected.

[11] The term "homeless" is based on how it is defined in Section 725 of the McKinney-Vento Homeless Assistance Act (42 U.S.C. 11434a).

[12] See College Opportunity and Affordability Act of 2008 (H.R. 4137/P.L. 110-315); A Place to Call Home Act (H.R. 3409); Energy Conservation Corps Act of 2008 (H.R. 7040); Transportation Job Corps Act of 2008 (H.R. 7053); and a bill to expand the work opportunity tax credit to include "disconnected youth" (H.R. 7066).

[13] For further information about the TRIO programs, *see Trio and GEAR UP Programs: Status and Issues*, by Jeffrey J. Kuenzi.

[14] U.S. Congress, House Committee on Rules, *Conference Report to Accompany H.R. 1 - The American Recovery and Reinvestment Act of 2009*, 110th Cong., 1st sess., February 8, 2009, Joint Explanatory Statement Division A and Division B.

[15] The 111th and 112th Congress have introduced bills that would address disconnected youth, including some bills that provide a definition of "disconnected."

[16] Some of the studies do not provide detailed information about the methodology used.

[17] Andrew Sum et al., *Left Behind in the Labor Market: Labor Market Problems of the Nation's Out-of-School, Young Adult Populations*, Northeastern University, Center for Labor Market Studies, Boston, 2003.

[18] A few studies, such as *The Condition of Education* (2007), by the Department of Education, and *What is Happening to Youth Employment Rates?* (2004), by the Congressional Budget

Office, do not use the term "disconnected" but evaluate the number and characteristics of youth who are not working or in school.

[19] Thomas MaCurdy, Bryan Keating, and Sriniketh Suryasesha, *Profiling the Plight of Disconnected Youth in America*, Stanford University, for the William and Hewlett Foundation, March 2006.

[20] Peter Edelman, Harry J. Holzer, and Paul Offner, *Reconnecting Disadvantaged Young Men* (Washington, DC: Urban Institute, 2006).

[21] Thomas MaCurdy, Bryan Keating, and Sriniketh Suryasesha, *Profiling the Plight of Disconnected Youth in America*, Stanford University, for the William and Hewlett Foundation, March 2006.

[22] Annie E. Casey Foundation, *Kids Count*, 2011; and Susan Jekielek and Brett Brown, *The Transition to Adulthood: Characteristics of Young Adults Ages 18 to 24 in America*, Annie E. Casey Foundation, Population Reference Bureau, and Child Trends, November 2005.

[23] Peter Edelman, Harry J. Holzer, and Paul Offner, *Reconnecting Disadvantaged Young Men* (Washington, DC: Urban Institute, 2006); and Congressional Budget Office, *What is Happening to Youth Employment Rates?*, November 2004.

[24] Michael Wald and Tia Martinez, *Connected by 25: Improving the Life Chances of the Country's Most Vulnerable 14-24 Year Olds*, Stanford University, for the William and Flora Hewlett Foundation, November 2003.

[25] U.S. Department of Education, National Center for Education Statistics, *The Condition of Education*, 2007.

[26] Andrew Sum et al., *Left Behind in the Labor Market: Labor Market Problems of the Nation's Out-of-School, Young Adult Populations*, Northeastern University, Center for Labor Market Studies, Boston, 2003.

[27] Annie E. Casey Foundation, *Kids Count Data Book*, 2011

[28] Thomas MaCurdy, Bryan Keating, and Sriniketh Suryasesha, *Profiling the Plight of Disconnected Youth in America.*

[29] Brett V. Brown and Carol Emig, "Prevalence, Patterns, and Outcomes," in *America's Disconnected Youth: Toward a Preventative Strategy*, ed. Douglas J. Besharov (Washington, DC: Child Welfare League of America, 1999).

[30] Congressional Budget Office, *What is Happening to Youth Employment Rates?*, November 2004.

[31] Reciprocally, youth who are not in school or working, married to a connected partner, *and not a parent* are considered disconnected.

[32] For additional information about the transition to adulthood, see CRS Report RL33975, *Vulnerable Youth: Background and Policies*, by Adrienne L. Fernandes-Alcantara.

[33] The limited research on runaway and homeless youth has found that these youth face challenges remaining in school and working. See Marjorie J. Robertson and Paul A. Toro, *Homeless Youth: Research, Intervention, and Policy*, U.S. Department of Health and Human Services, Office of the Assistant Secretary for Planning and Evaluation, The 1998 National Symposium on Homeless Research, 1998.

[34] For a discussion of social networks in low-income communities, see Katherine S. Newman, *No Shame In My Game: The Working Poor in the Inner City*, (New York: Vintage Books and Russell Sage Foundation, 1999), pp. 72-84.

[35] Brett V. Brown and Carol Emig, "Prevalence, Patterns, and Outcomes," in Douglass J. Besharov, ed. *America's Disconnected Youth: Toward a Preventative Strategy* (Washington, D.C.: Child Welfare League of America, 1999). See also, Douglas J.

Besharov and Karen N Gardiner, "Introduction" in Douglas J. Besharov, ed. *America's Disconnected Youth: Toward a Preventative Strategy.*

[36] The CPS asks several questions to determine whether individuals are considered to have a work disability. Persons are identified as having a work disability if they: (1) reported having a health problem or disability which prevents them from working or which limits the kind or amount of work they can do; or (2) ever retired or left a job for health reasons; or (3) did not work in the survey week because of long-term physical or mental illness or disability which prevents the performance of any kind of work; or (4) did not work at all in the previous year because they were ill or disabled; or (5) are under 65 years of age and covered by Medicare; or (6) are under age 65 years of age and a recipient of Supplemental Security Income (SSI); or (7) received veteran's disability compensation. Persons are considered to have a severe work disability if they meet any of the criteria in 3 through 6, above. See http://www.census.gov/hhes/ www/disability/disabcps.html.

[37] Individuals who receive Social Security disability are eligible to receive Medicare two years after entitlement to SSDI, and in some cases earlier. Disabled children may receive Social Security Disability Insurance (SSDI) benefits indefinitely as long as the disability was incurred before reaching age 22. For information about SSDI, see CRS Report RL32279, *Primer on Disability Benefits: Social Security Disability Insurance (SSDI) and Supplemental Security Income (SSI)*, by Umar Moulta-Ali.

[38] This is based on the status dropout rate, or the dropout rate regardless of when an individual dropped out. Separately, the event dropout rate refers to the share of youth who dropped out within a given school year. The event dropout rate for males and females is similar. U.S. Department of Education, National Center for Education Statistics, "Percentage of high school dropouts among persons 16 through 24 years old (status dropout rate), by sex and race/ethnicity: Selected years, 1960 through 2009," August 2010, http://nces.ed.gov /programs/digest/d10/tables/dt10_115.asp.

[39] The social science literature has discussed the challenges that males, particularly men of color in urban communities, face in staying connected to work. See for example, Peter Edelman, Harry J. Holzer, and Paul Offner, *Reconnecting Disadvantaged Young Men* (Washington, D.C.: Urban Institute Press, 2006) and William Julius Wilson, *When Work Disappears: The World of the New Urban Poor* (New York: Vintage Books, 1996). See also, CRS Report R41431, *Child Well-Being and Noncustodial Fathers*, by Carmen Solomon-Fears, Gene Falk, and Adrienne L. FernandesAlcantara.

[40] In this analysis, disconnected youth with children are unmarried or are married to a disconnected partner. Children include biological children, adoptive children, or step-children who live in the same home as the disconnected individual.

[41] Asian or Pacific Islander and Native Americans and Alaskan Natives are not included in this analysis; however, these groups are included in the "other" category of Table 1 and in select tables in Appendix B.

[42] U.S. Department of Labor, Bureau of Labor Statistics, *Education Pays*, May 4, 2011.

[43] Data are 2008 annual averages for persons age 25 and over. Earnings are for full-time wage and salary workers.

[44] Census Bureau, "Poverty Thresholds," http://www.census.gov/hhes/www/poverty /data/threshld/.

[45] For further discussion, CRS Report RL32237, *Health Insurance: A Primer*, by Bernadette Fernandez.

[46] Carmen DeNavas-Walt, Bernadette D. Proctor, and Jessica C. Smith, *Income, Poverty, and Health Insurance in the United States: 2010*, U.S. Census Bureau, Current Population Reports, September 2011, p. 24.

[47] Social Security Administration, *Medicaid Information*, http://www.socialsecurity.gov /disabilityresearch/wi/ medicaid.htm.

[48] Under the Patient Protection and Affordable Care Act (P.L. 111-148), health plans that provide dependent coverage must extend that existing coverage to children under the age of 26. However, certain health plans are exempt from this requirement if the adult child has an offer of coverage from his/her own employer. For further information, see CRS Report R41220, *Preexisting Exclusion Provisions for Children and Dependent Coverage under the Patient Protection and Affordable Care Act (PPACA)*, by Hinda Chaikind and Bernadette Fernandez.

[49] *On the Frontier of Adulthood: Theory, Research, and Public Policy*, ed. Richard A. Settersten, Jr., Frank F. Furstenburg, Jr., and Rubén Rumbaut (Chicago: University of Chicago, 2005).

[50] U.S. Government Accountability Office, *Disconnected Youth: Federal Action Could Address Some of the Challenges Faced by Local Programs That Reconnect Youth Education and Employment*, GAO-08-313, February 2008, p. 1.

[51] For further discussion of the influence of family structure on socioeconomic outcomes and financial well-being in adulthood, see CRS Report RL34756, *Nonmarital Childbearing: Trends, Reasons, and Public Policy Interventions*, by Carmen Solomon-Fears.

[52] For further information, see CRS Report R41431, *Child Well-Being and Noncustodial Fathers*, by Carmen Solomon-Fears, Gene Falk, and Adrienne L. Fernandes-Alcantara.

[53] Prior to the 2007 CPS, it was possible only to directly link a child to one of his/her parents. In cases where the parents were married, the child could be linked through the one parent to that parent's spouse. For the time-series data presented here, this method is applied in all years in the series (i.e., 1988 through 2011). Beginning in 2007, the Census Bureau refined its procedures for identifying and linking children with their parent(s). Under the new procedures, one can identify both the mother and father directly, if residing in the household with the child, and determine whether the parent is a biological parent, a step-parent, or an adoptive parent. It is this later definition that is used in the cross-sectional data for 2008, presented earlier. Using this procedure, a child's parents are identifiable regardless of whether the parents are married.

[54] See, for example: Susan E. Mayer, *What Money Can't Buy: Family Income and Children's Life Chances* (Cambridge, Massachusetts: Harvard University Press, 1997) and Greg J. Duncan and Jeanne Brooks-Gunn (eds.), *Consequences of Growing Up Poor* (New York: Russell Sage Foundation, 1997).

[55] Phillip Kaufman et al., *Dropout Rates in the United States: 1998*, Department of Education, National Center for Education Statistics, Statistical Analysis Report NCES 2000-022, November 1999, p. 55.

[56] See, Jay D. Teachman et al., "Poverty During Adolescence and Subsequent Educational Attainment," in *Consequences of Growing Up Poor*, ibid, pp. 382-418.

[57] Ibid., p. 413.

[58] Robert Haveman and Barbara Wolfe, "Schooling and Fertility Outcomes: Reduced-Form and Structural Estimates," in *Childhood Poverty and Adolescent Consequences of Growing Up Poor*, op cit., p. 442.

[59] Ibid., p. 443.

[60] For further information about the role of these factors in childhood development, see CRS Report RL33975, *Vulnerable Youth: Background and Policies*, by Adrienne L. Fernandes-Alcantara.

[61] Healther Koball et al., *Syntehsis of Research and Resources to Support at-Risk Youth*, Mathematica Policy Research, Inc., ACF Youth Demonstration Development Project, June 21, 2011..

[62] James J. Heckman and Dimitriy V. Masterov, *The Productivity of Investing in Young Children*, 2007.

[63] See, Rhonda Tsoi-A-Fatt, *A Collective Responsibility, A Collective Work: Supporting the Path to Positive Life Outcomes for Youth in Economically Distressed Communities*, Center for Law and Social Policy, May 2008.

[64] The Harlem Children's Zone in New York is one such model that provides wrap-around services for children of all ages. Services include parenting courses, community services, educational programs at HCZ charters schools, and foster care prevention services, among other services.

[65] For an overview of federal programs and policies to assist vulnerable youth across several domains, including workforce development, education, juvenile justice and delinquency prevention, social services, public health, and national and community service, see CRS Report RL33975, *Vulnerable Youth: Background and Policies*, by Adrienne L. Fernandes-Alcantara.

[66] See for example, Nancy Martin and Samuel Halperin, "Whatever It Takes: How Twelve Communities Are Reconnecting Out-of-School Youth," American Youth Policy Forum, 2006; National League of Cities, "Beyond City Limits: Cross-System Collaboration to Reengage Disconnected Youth," 2007; and U.S. Government Accountability Office, *Disconnected Youth: Federal Action Could Address Some of the Challenges Faced by Local Programs That Reconnect Youth Education and Employment*, GAO-08-313, February 2008.

[67] For further discussion, see CRS Report RL34756, *Nonmarital Childbearing: Trends, Reasons, and Public Policy Interventions*, by Carmen Solomon-Fears.

INDEX

A

academic success, 37
access, 21, 22, 30, 39, 41, 48, 49, 51, 67, 86, 105
accessibility, 30, 41, 50
accountability, 2, 7, 24, 25, 41, 47
accounting, 76
ACF, 143
action research, 28
additional schooling, 82, 91
adolescents, 107
adulthood, 69, 75, 83, 92, 107, 108, 110, 111, 142
adults, 31, 48, 50, 54
advancement, 36
advocacy, 29, 45
African Americans, 14
age, 2, 31, 70, 71, 72, 73, 74, 75, 76, 80, 83, 86, 87, 93, 101, 110, 116, 117, 138, 141, 142
agencies, 6, 22, 24, 25, 26, 41, 71
Alaska, 113, 117
ambassadors, 57
American Recovery and Reinvestment Act, 35, 70, 139
American Recovery and Reinvestment Act of 2009, 70, 139
appropriations, 138
armed forces, 72, 75, 112, 113, 115, 117

arrest, 13
aspiration, 52
assessment, 7, 29, 44
assets, 15, 21, 48
AT&T, 55
attachment, viii, 65, 76, 84, 102
authority(s), 28, 41, 45
aversion, 52
avoidance, 111
awareness, 1, 2, 6, 7, 30, 35, 44, 47, 48, 57

B

barriers, 20, 22
base, 6, 36, 86, 99, 100, 109
base rate, 99, 100, 109
behaviors, 110
beneficiaries, 8
benefits, 7, 32, 40, 43, 47, 67, 76, 83, 109, 110, 141
birth rate, 12, 109
births, 108
black women, 109
blueprint, 26
bounds, 21
Brittany, 4
building blocks, 55
Bureau of Justice Statistics, 114, 139
Bureau of Labor Statistics, 141
businesses, 6, 26, 49, 55, 56, 57, 58, 70

F

G